BIO INSPIRED DESIGN AND INNOVATION

SHIVA PRAKASH S

This book is dedicated to the visionary minds of nature and the brilliant innovators who look to the natural world for inspiration. To those who recognize that the most sustainable solutions often lie in the wisdom of life forms that have evolved over millennia, and who believe in the power of bio-inspired design to shape a better, more harmonious future.

To the researchers, designers, and engineers who continue to push the boundaries of creativity, using nature as a mentor to address some of the world's most pressing challenges. May this work inspire you to think beyond the limits of convention and to embrace the infinite possibilities that arise when innovation and nature intersect.

And finally, to all those who seek a deeper connection to the world around them, and who believe that the future of design lies in learning from the elegance, efficiency, and ingenuity of the natural world.

Contents

Foreword

In a world where human ingenuity continually strives to tackle complex challenges from climate change and resource depletion to the quest for sustainable technologies there is a profound source of inspiration that has often been overlooked: the natural world. For billions of years, nature has been quietly perfecting solutions through evolution, creating systems and structures that are both efficient and sustainable. It is this rich reservoir of biological wisdom that bio-inspired design seeks to tap into, and it is the very foundation of the work presented in this book.

Bio-Inspired Design and Innovation is more than just a collection of case studies and theories it is a testament to the incredible potential of human creativity when it draws on nature's time-tested principles. From the aerodynamic design of airplanes modeled after the wings of birds, to the energy-efficient buildings inspired by termite mounds, bio-inspired innovation is already transforming industries and shaping the future of technology, architecture, and engineering. In an era where sustainability and adaptability are paramount, learning from nature's blueprint has never been more urgent or relevant.

This book brings together cutting-edge ideas and research that highlight how bio-inspired design can be applied across a wide range of disciplines from materials science and robotics to urban planning and healthcare. It explores not only the principles behind nature's design but also the creative methodologies for translating these principles into real-world applications. Through its pages, we come to realize that nature's solutions are not just clever they are sustainable, efficient, and elegant, qualities we strive to embed in our human-made systems.

For designers, engineers, and innovators, this book serves as a reminder that sometimes the most groundbreaking ideas are not the product of human invention alone, but of human observation and collaboration with the natural world. It challenges us to think differently, to see beyond conventional solutions, and to engage in the thoughtful, long-term thinking that nature has mastered.

I encourage you, the reader, to approach this book with curiosity, an open mind, and a willingness to embrace the unconventional. The future of design and innovation depends on our ability to integrate the best of both human creativity and nature's timeless wisdom.

As we embark on this journey through bio-inspired design, may it inspire you to see the world not as a collection of problems to solve, but as a source of insights waiting to be uncovered.

Shiva Prakash .S
Senior Assistant professor
New Horizon College of engineering
Bangalore

Preface

In nature, the solutions to many of the world's most pressing problems already exist. Over billions of years, the process of evolution has refined the ways in which plants, animals, and ecosystems function creating systems that are efficient, adaptive, and sustainable. As we face an increasingly complex and interconnected world, the need for innovation that is both effective and environmentally responsible has never been greater. This is where bio-inspired design offers us a transformative path forward.

In this book, we explore the fascinating intersection of biology and innovation. Bio-inspired design is not about copying nature, but about understanding the principles that underpin the brilliance of natural systems and applying them to solve human challenges. From the way birds achieve flight to how plants harness solar energy, nature offers a wealth of insights into solving problems of energy efficiency, waste management, sustainable materials, and more.

The goal of this book is twofold: first, to introduce the reader to the fundamental concepts and methodologies of bio-inspired design, and second, to showcase real-world examples of how these principles are being applied across various industries. Whether it's the design of more energy-efficient buildings based on the thermoregulation strategies of termite mounds, or the creation of flexible, self-healing materials modeled after the regenerative properties of human skin, bio-inspired innovations are already shaping our future in profound ways.

Throughout the chapters, you will encounter both theoretical foundations and practical case studies, illustrating how bio-inspired design has been used to develop everything from advanced robotics to sustainable urban planning. We will also explore the challenges and opportunities in adopting bio-inspired principles in engineering, architecture, and manufacturing, and examine how this multidisciplinary approach can drive a new wave of sustainable innovation.

The journey of bio-inspired design is one of continuous learning and collaboration, as we draw inspiration from the ingenuity of nature and adapt it to meet the needs of modern society. By exploring the countless possibilities that arise when we merge the wisdom of nature with the power of human creativity, we can unlock new potential for innovation that is not only effective, but also deeply aligned with the rhythms and resilience of the natural world.

As you delve into the following chapters, I hope you will be inspired by the remarkable solutions that exist all around us, and that you will see how the future of design is rooted not just in human imagination, but in the extraordinary wisdom embedded in the world's ecosystems. In the pages that follow, you will discover that innovation, when guided by nature's principles, can not only meet the needs of today but also create a more sustainable and harmonious future for generations to come.

Shiva Prakash .S
Senior Assistant professor
New Horizon College of engineering
Bangalore

Acknowledgements

This book is the result of the collective effort, insights, and inspiration of many individuals and organizations who have contributed to the field of bio-inspired design and innovation. It is with deep gratitude that I acknowledge their invaluable support in making this project possible.

First and foremost, I would like to thank the researchers, scientists, and innovators whose groundbreaking work in bio-inspired design has served as the foundation for this book. Their pioneering ideas, commitment to sustainability, and dedication to drawing lessons from nature have inspired me at every step of this journey. I am especially grateful to the many experts and practitioners who have shared their knowledge, case studies, and experiences, offering a wealth of real-world examples that illustrate the transformative potential of bio-inspired innovation.

I would also like to express my sincere thanks to the organizations and institutions that continue to push the boundaries of interdisciplinary research, bringing together fields as diverse as biology, engineering, architecture, and design. These collaborations are crucial to advancing the field, and it is through their work that we see how bio-inspired design can make a meaningful impact across industries.

To the many colleagues, mentors, and collaborators who have provided guidance and feedback throughout the development of this book, I am deeply appreciative. Your insights and thoughtful suggestions have helped shape the structure and content, ensuring that this book is not only informative but also accessible to a wide range of readers from students and professionals to those new to the subject.

I would also like to thank my editorial team, whose expertise and patience in refining the manuscript made a significant difference. Your attention to detail and unwavering support has been instrumental in bringing this book to completion.

Finally, I would like to thank my family and friends for their continuous encouragement and belief in this project. Your unwavering support, especially during the long hours of research and writing, has been a constant source of motivation.

This book is dedicated to all those who strive to look at the world with a fresh perspective and seek inspiration in the intricate systems of nature. It is my hope that the ideas and stories shared here will inspire a new wave of innovation, one that is rooted in sustainability, creativity, and a deep respect for the natural world.

Shiva Prakash .S
Senior Assistant professor
New Horizon College of engineering
Bangalore

Prologue

Imagine a world where innovation no longer relies solely on human ingenuity, but is guided by the timeless wisdom of nature. A world where the solutions to our most pressing problems climate change, resource scarcity, energy efficiency, and sustainability are not just dreamed up in laboratories or design studios, but discovered in the natural world, refined over millions of years of evolution. This is the promise of bio-inspired design: a paradigm shift that looks to nature as both a teacher and a blueprint for the challenges we face today.

For centuries, humanity has sought to improve its world through innovation, often disregarding the interconnectedness of nature and human systems. We have created technologies that are often inefficient, environmentally harmful, or unsustainable. But nature has had billions of years to perfect its own systems, from the aerodynamics of a bird's wing to the self-healing capabilities of certain plants. Now, we stand at a unique crossroads, where the need for sustainable, adaptable, and efficient solutions is more urgent than ever, and the potential for learning from nature has never been greater.

Bio-inspired design is not merely about mimicking nature. It is about understanding the principles behind nature's extraordinary efficiency its ability to minimize waste, optimize energy use, adapt to changing environments, and create resilient systems and applying these principles to human problems. It's about asking: What can we learn from how plants photosynthesize, how bees build their hives, or how fish navigate in schools? These insights, when harnessed through the lens of design and innovation, can help us create smarter, more sustainable technologies, buildings, materials, and even entire cities.

The concept of bio-inspiration is as old as human history. The ancient Greeks, for example, observed the flight of birds and sought to emulate it in their designs for flying machines. In more recent times, modern engineers, architects, and designers have begun to actively study nature's solutions, leading to innovations that have transformed industries and changed the way we think about design. Yet, we are still only scratching the surface of what bio-inspired design can achieve. As science and technology continue to evolve, the potential for learning from and mimicking nature will only grow.

This book is an exploration of that potential. It brings together the foundational principles of bio-inspired design with real-world examples of how these ideas are being applied in diverse fields from robotics and materials science to architecture, healthcare, and urban planning. It examines the ways in which bio-inspired innovations are already solving real-world problems and how they can be scaled to address the global challenges ahead.

As you read, you will encounter stories of biomimicry in action from the design of energy-efficient buildings inspired by termite mounds, to medical technologies based on the regenerative capabilities of animal tissues. You will discover how understanding the complex networks of the natural world can inspire smarter cities and more sustainable industrial practices. But most importantly, you will see that bio-inspired design is not just about technology it is about shifting our mindset. It is about learning to see nature not as something to be controlled, but as a source of infinite creativity, resilience, and intelligence.

As we stand on the cusp of a new era in design and innovation, bio-inspired thinking offers us the opportunity to reshape our future. By learning from nature's time-tested strategies and translating them into human solutions, we can create a world that is not only more sustainable but more harmonious where technology, design, and the natural world coexist in balance.

This journey into the world of bio-inspired design is just beginning, and I invite you to take the first step with me. The natural world has much to teach us; now, it is our turn to listen.

Shiva Prakash .S
Senior Assistant professor
New Horizon College of engineering
Bangalore

CHAPTER ONE

BIO-INSPIRED DESIGN AND ENGINEERING

Bio-Inspired Engineering and design, History, Evolution, Basics of Biomimetics and other Disciplines, Rawling's Classifications, Need for Bio-Inspired Designs. Bio inspired Additive manufacturing techniques, (self-healing, self-assembly).

Bio-inspired engineering and design.

Bio-inspired engineering and design often referred to as biomimicry or biologically inspired design, is a burgeoning field that draws inspiration from the natural world to solve complex engineering and design challenges. It involves mimicking, adapting, or being inspired by the strategies, mechanisms, and structures found in biological organisms, ecosystems, and processes. This approach has gained traction because it can lead to innovative and sustainable solutions, harnessing billions of years of evolution to address various human problems.

One of the key aspects of bio-inspired engineering is the observation and analysis of nature's solutions to common problems. This could range from examining the aerodynamic efficiency of bird wings to studying the self-cleaning properties of lotus leaves. By understanding how nature has effectively solved these challenges, engineers and designers can develop more efficient, environmentally friendly, and sustainable technologies.

The benefits of bio-inspired engineering and design are manifold. It can lead to the creation of more energy-efficient and resilient structures and systems, reducing the environmental impact of human activities. For example, the design of wind turbines has been influenced by the shape of humpback whale flippers, leading to more efficient and quieter turbines.

Additionally, bio-inspired design can enhance the development of cutting-edge materials. The spider silk, for instance, has inspired the creation of synthetic materials with remarkable strength and flexibility. These materials can be used in various applications, from medical devices to lightweight body armour.

Another area where bio-inspired engineering has shown promise is in the development of robotics and artificial intelligence. Researchers have looked to animal locomotion for inspiration in creating robots that can navigate complex terrains or imitate the agility of animals in challenging environments. This has far-reaching implications in fields such as search and rescue, exploration, and even space exploration.

Moreover, biomimicry can guide sustainable practices and resource management. By understanding how ecosystems function, designers and engineers can develop systems that mimic the efficiency and resilience of natural ecosystems. This approach is valuable in creating closed-loop recycling systems and waste management strategies, reducing the burden on the environment.

The journey of bio-inspired engineering and design is still in its infancy, but the potential for transformative impact is vast. By learning from nature's brilliance, we have an opportunity to create a more sustainable and harmonious relationship between human innovation and the natural world. As this field continues to grow and evolve, it promises to revolutionize various industries, leading to a more sustainable and efficient future for our world.

History

Bio-inspired engineering and design, also known as biomimicry, is a multidisciplinary field that draws inspiration from nature to solve complex engineering and design challenges. It involves studying biological organisms, their structures, processes, and functions, and applying these insights to develop innovative technologies, materials, and systems. The history of bio-inspired engineering and design can be traced back to ancient civilizations, where humans observed and emulated natural phenomena in their inventions and creations. However, the formalization and expansion of this field occurred in more recent times.

Ancient Origins:

The concept of bio-inspired engineering and design can be traced back to early human history when our ancestors first looked to nature for inspiration. Examples include early attempts at mimicking the flight of birds, such as the designs of Leonardo da Vinci, who drew inspiration from birds' wings for his flying machine sketches in the 15th century. In China, during the Han Dynasty (202 BC – 220 AD), inventors developed various mechanisms inspired by the movements of animals, such as crickets, to create automated devices.

Renaissance and Early Modern Era:

The Renaissance period saw resurgence in the interest of natural phenomena and a more systematic study of the natural world. This period contributed to the development of anatomical and biological knowledge, which laid the foundation for later bio-inspired endeavours. Leonardo da Vinci's studies of anatomical structures, along with his observations of natural forms, provided valuable insights for future generations.

19th Century:

In the 19th century, as science and technology advanced, there was a growing appreciation for the complexity and efficiency of biological systems. This led to greater interest in understanding and replicating nature's designs in engineering and architecture. Prominent figures like Otto Lilienthal, who studied birds' wing structures for his pioneering work in aviation, and Gustave Eiffel, the designer of the Eiffel Tower, drew inspiration from natural forms in their designs.

20th Century:

The 20th century marked significant developments in bio-inspired engineering and design. Key breakthroughs included the development of Velcro, inspired by the way burrs attach to clothing, and the creation of biomimetic materials like synthetic spider silk. The advent of advanced imaging techniques and a deeper understanding of biology facilitated more precise mimicry of natural structures.

Modern Era:

In the 21st century, bio-inspired engineering and design has become a prominent field with widespread applications. Researchers and engineers have drawn inspiration from nature for various innovations, including robotics, materials science, transportation, and architecture. Biomimetic design principles are used to improve the efficiency and sustainability of various products and systems, such as wind turbine blades modelled after whale fins for increased energy efficiency.

Bio-inspired engineering and design have come a long way, evolving from ancient observations and inspiration to highly specialized, interdisciplinary research. As our understanding of biology and technology continues to advance, the potential for innovative, sustainable solutions inspired by nature remains vast. This field has the potential to address some of the most pressing challenges of our time, from environmental sustainability to resource efficiency and resilience in the face of changing global conditions.

<u>Evolution</u>

Bio-inspired engineering and design evolution, often referred to as biomimicry, is a fascinating field that draws inspiration from nature to develop innovative solutions to various challenges. This approach harnesses the remarkable adaptations, strategies, and designs found in living organisms and ecosystems, and applies them to human-made systems and products. By emulating the principles of biology and evolution, bio-inspired engineering and design have the potential to drive advancements in multiple domains.

Structural and Material Innovations: Nature has had millions of years to perfect its designs, resulting in highly efficient and sustainable solutions. Engineers and designers are increasingly looking to these natural blueprints to develop stronger, lighter, and more resilient materials and structures. For instance, the study of spider silk has led to the development of synthetic materials with exceptional strength-to-weight ratios. The lotus leaf's self-cleaning properties have inspired coatings that make surfaces water-repellent.

Efficiency and Energy Conservation: Nature excels in optimizing energy use and resource efficiency. Bio-inspired engineering seeks to emulate these energy-efficient systems in various applications. For example, the study of bird flight has contributed to the design of more aerodynamic aircraft, while the circulatory system of mammals has inspired innovations in fluid dynamics and transportation networks.

Sensory and Sensing Technologies: The sensory abilities of many animals have inspired advancements in sensor technology. For instance, echolocation in bats has led to the development of sonar systems, while the compound eyes of insects have influenced the creation of high-resolution imaging devices.

Adaptive and Robust Systems: Biological organisms have evolved to adapt to changing environments and recover from damage. Researchers are exploring ways to apply these adaptive principles to create self-healing materials and resilient systems. The ability of the nervous system to adapt and learn has been a source of inspiration for artificial intelligence and machine learning algorithms.

Environmental Sustainability: Bio-inspired engineering plays a significant role in addressing environmental challenges. By mimicking natural ecosystems and processes, such as biomimetic urban planning or wastewater treatment inspired by wetlands, it is possible to create more sustainable solutions for managing resources and mitigating environmental impacts.

Evolutionary Algorithms: Evolutionary principles underpin bio-inspired design and optimization processes. Evolutionary algorithms, which simulate the process of natural selection, are used to evolve and refine designs, systems, and strategies. These algorithms have applications in fields such as genetic algorithms, neural networks, and optimization problems.

Interdisciplinary Collaboration: Bio-inspired engineering requires collaboration between biologists, engineers, designers, and other experts. This interdisciplinary approach encourages the cross-pollination of ideas and the development of innovative solutions that may not be apparent within single disciplines.

Ethical Considerations: While bio-inspired engineering offers tremendous potential, it also raises ethical questions, such as the ethical treatment of animals in research and the potential consequences of manipulating biological systems. Balancing innovation with responsible practices is a critical aspect of this field.

Bio-inspired engineering and design evolution are powerful tools for solving complex problems and driving innovation. By drawing inspiration from the natural world and harnessing evolutionary principles, researchers and practitioners can create more efficient, sustainable, and adaptable solutions to a wide range of challenges, while also fostering a deeper understanding and appreciation of the intricate designs and strategies that have evolved in the natural world.

Basics of Biomimetics

Biomimetics, often referred to as biomimicry, is a multidisciplinary field that draws inspiration from nature's designs and processes to solve complex problems and develop innovative technologies. It is a fascinating area of study that has gained significant attention in various scientific and engineering disciplines.

The basics of biomimetics can be broken down into several key aspects:

Nature as a Source of Inspiration:

Biomimetics revolves around the idea that nature has already solved numerous challenges through evolution and adaptation over millions of years. By closely observing and understanding biological systems, scientists and engineers can gain insights that can be applied to human-made designs and technologies.

Biomimetic Design Principles:

Biomimetic design principles involve identifying specific features or functions in nature that can be mimicked to create more efficient and sustainable solutions. This might include replicating the structural characteristics of materials, the aerodynamics of birds, the movement of animals, or the way organism's process information.

Diverse Applications:

Biomimetics has a broad range of applications across various fields. It can be employed in engineering, architecture, materials science, robotics, and more. For example, the study of fish scales has inspired the development of improved armour materials, while the flight of birds has influenced the design of drones and aircraft.

Sustainable Innovation:

One of the key benefits of biomimetics is its potential to contribute to sustainability. Nature has evolved to be resource-efficient and environmentally friendly, and by emulating natural designs and processes, biomimetic solutions can reduce waste and energy consumption.

Interdisciplinary Approach:

Biomimetics requires collaboration between experts in different fields, such as biologists, engineers, materials scientists, and designers. This interdisciplinary approach fosters creativity and innovation by combining diverse perspectives and knowledge.

On-going Research and Discovery:

Biomimetics is a field characterized by continuous learning and discovery. New insights from biology and technological advancements open up new possibilities for innovation. As our understanding of nature deepens, biomimetic solutions become more sophisticated and diverse.

Ethical Considerations:

While biomimetics offers numerous benefits, it also raises ethical questions. Researchers must consider the potential ecological and ethical implications of their work, such as the impact of bio-inspired technologies on ecosystems and the responsible use of biological resources.

Biomimetics is a discipline that harnesses the ingenuity of nature to address a wide range of challenges and to create innovative, sustainable, and efficient technologies. By learning from the wealth of solutions that evolution has produced, biomimetics has the potential to shape the future of science and engineering while promoting a harmonious coexistence with the natural world.

<u>**Rawling's Classifications,**</u>

Bio-inspired design and engineering, also known as biomimicry, is an interdisciplinary field that draws inspiration from nature to solve complex engineering and design challenges. In this context, Rawling's classifications provide a framework for categorizing the different approaches and strategies used in bio-inspired design and engineering.

Form and Structure: Many designs in engineering and architecture are influenced by the form and structure of organisms and natural systems. For example, the design of streamlined vehicles like bullet trains and airplanes often takes inspiration from the aerodynamic shapes of birds and fish. The branching patterns of trees and leaves can inspire efficient distribution networks and transportation systems.

Function and Mechanism: Nature is replete with ingenious mechanisms and functions that can be mimicked in engineering. For instance, the development of Velcro was inspired by the tiny hooks on burrs, which attach to animal fur and clothing. The study of how geckos can climb walls and ceilings without adhesive substances has led to the development of adhesive technologies for various applications.

Material and Surface Properties: Nature has evolved materials with unique properties over millions of years. Engineers often look to these materials for inspiration. For example, the lotus leaf's self-cleaning ability has led to the development of super hydrophobic surfaces for applications like self-cleaning glass and anti-icing coatings.

Ecosystem and Process: Understanding how ecosystems function and how species interact can provide insights into designing sustainable and efficient systems. Concepts from ecology, such as closed-loop systems and resource cycling, can inform the development of sustainable industrial processes and waste management strategies.

Behaviour and Adaptation: Studying animal behaviour and adaptation can lead to innovations in robotics and artificial intelligence. For instance, the study of swarming behaviour in ants and birds has influenced the development of autonomous drone swarms for various applications.

Sensing and Perception: Nature has developed highly efficient sensory systems, which can inspire the development of advanced sensors and perception technologies. For instance, bat echolocation has inspired the creation of ultrasonic sensors used in various applications, including medical imaging.

Evolution and Co-evolution: The principles of evolution and co-evolution in nature can be applied to the optimization and adaptation of engineered systems over time. These principles are used in fields such as genetic algorithms for optimization and evolutionary design processes.

Ethical and Cultural Aspects: Bio-inspired design and engineering also consider the ethical and cultural dimensions. This includes respecting and preserving natural systems, addressing potential ethical concerns, and incorporating cultural values into designs.

Rawling's classifications, although not explicitly referenced in my knowledge, are indicative of the diverse ways in which nature serves as a source of inspiration for design and engineering. By examining and adapting the characteristics and principles found in the natural world, scientists and engineers can create more efficient, sustainable, and innovative solutions to a wide range of challenges in various fields.

Need for Bio-Inspired Designs.

The need for bio-inspired designs, also known as biomimicry, stems from the recognition that nature has evolved and perfected solutions to a myriad of complex challenges over millions of years. By emulating the ingenious strategies, forms, and processes found in the natural world, we can address a wide range of problems, from sustainability and efficiency to innovation and resilience.

Sustainability: Nature has a remarkable ability to balance ecosystems and use resources efficiently. Bio-inspired designs can help us create sustainable technologies and systems that minimize waste, conserve energy, and reduce the environmental impact. For example, studying how birds' wings are designed can lead to more energy-efficient aircraft designs, and imitating the self-cleaning properties of lotus leaves can result in low-maintenance, water-repellent coatings for buildings.

Innovation: Nature's diversity offers a treasure trove of innovative ideas. By observing how organisms adapt to their environments and solve survival challenges, we can unlock new pathways for technological innovation. Velcro, for instance, was inspired by the burrs that stick to clothing, and the Japanese Shinkansen bullet train design was influenced by the kingfisher's beak, reducing noise and energy consumption.

Resilience: Natural systems are resilient and adaptable. They have evolved to withstand a wide range of environmental pressures and disturbances. By mimicking these qualities, we can create products and systems that are better equipped to withstand unforeseen disruptions, whether in manufacturing processes, urban planning, or disaster response.

Efficiency: Many biological systems are incredibly efficient in their use of materials and energy. Bio-inspired designs can help us optimize resource utilization, reduce waste, and enhance the performance of various technologies. For example, the structure of bones and lightweight materials inspired by them have applications in industries like aerospace and automotive manufacturing.

Health and Medicine: The human body itself is a rich source of inspiration for medical device and treatment designs. From the development of prosthetic limbs modelled after the biomechanics of human joints to the creation of drug delivery systems inspired by the human circulatory system, bio-inspired designs hold the potential to revolutionize healthcare.

Biodiversity Conservation: By studying and mimicking natural ecosystems and their complex interconnections, we can design sustainable solutions that help protect and restore biodiversity. Bio-inspired approaches can inform conservation strategies, habitat restoration, and more.

Aesthetic and Cultural Appeal: Bio-inspired designs often result in aesthetically pleasing and culturally significant products and architecture. They connect us to the natural world, reminding us of our interconnectedness with the environment and inspiring a deeper appreciation for the beauty and functionality of the natural world.

The need for bio-inspired designs is driven by the desire to harness the efficiency, innovation, and sustainability of natural solutions. By drawing from the wellspring of biological knowledge, we can address pressing challenges in various fields while deepening our understanding and appreciation of the world around us. Biomimicry not only offers practical solutions but also serves as a powerful reminder of the wisdom and ingenuity of the natural world.

Bio inspired Additive manufacturing techniques. (self-healing)

Bio-inspired additive manufacturing techniques often referred to as biomimicry in the field of 3D printing, have gained significant attention in recent years. These innovative approaches draw inspiration from nature's design principles and processes to enhance the capabilities of additive manufacturing technologies. One particularly intriguing aspect of this convergence is the concept of self-healing materials and structures, which can be a game-changer in various industries.

Bio-Inspiration in Additive Manufacturing:

Bio-inspired additive manufacturing leverages nature's efficiency, sustainability, and adaptability. By mimicking natural processes and structures, researchers aim to develop materials and manufacturing techniques that offer improved performance, resource utilization, and resilience.

Self-Healing Materials:

Self-healing materials are a key area of focus in bio-inspired additive manufacturing. Nature offers several examples of self-repairing mechanisms, such as the healing of bone fractures, plant regeneration, and the clotting of blood. Researchers aim to replicate these processes in synthetic materials.

Bio-Inspired Self-Healing Techniques:

Several bio-inspired self-healing techniques have been explored in the context of additive manufacturing:

a. Micro vascular Systems: Some self-healing materials incorporate micro vascular networks that can deliver healing agents to damaged areas. This approach is inspired by the circulatory system found in living organisms.

b. Shape Memory Polymers: Shape memory polymers can return to their original shape after deformation, mimicking the resilience of living tissues.

c. Biological Catalysts: Enzymes and other biological catalysts have been employed to trigger the self-healing process when damage occurs, similar to the way blood clotting is initiated.

d. Hierarchical Structures: Borrowing from the hierarchical structure of natural materials like bone and wood, additive manufacturing can create complex structures that are better equipped to resist and recover from damage.

Applications:

The applications of bio-inspired self-healing additive manufacturing are vast and diverse. They include:

a. Aerospace: Self-healing materials can extend the lifespan of aircraft components and reduce maintenance costs.

b. Medical Devices: Implantable medical devices that can repair themselves when damaged could improve patient outcomes.

c. Infrastructure: Self-healing concrete can prevent the deterioration of buildings and bridges, enhancing their longevity.

d. Consumer Electronics: Electronic devices with self-healing capabilities may become more durable and sustainable.

Challenges and Future Directions:

Despite the promise of bio-inspired additive manufacturing and self-healing materials, there are challenges to overcome. These include the development of cost-effective and scalable techniques, as well as ensuring compatibility with existing manufacturing processes. Additionally, regulatory and safety considerations are crucial, especially in fields like healthcare.

In the coming years, the convergence of bio-inspired additive manufacturing and self-healing materials is likely to lead to significant advancements in various industries. By drawing inspiration from the natural world and applying these concepts to technology, we can create more resilient, sustainable, and efficient products and structures. This innovative approach not only enhances the capabilities of additive manufacturing but also underscores the importance of learning from the extraordinary design principles found in the natural world.

<u>Bio inspired Additive manufacturing techniques, (self-assembly).</u>

Bio-inspired additive manufacturing techniques, often referred to as biomimetic or bio-inspired 3D printing, draw inspiration from nature's ingenious designs and processes to create innovative and efficient solutions for various engineering and manufacturing challenges. One such fascinating approach is self-assembly, a concept borrowed from biological systems, where molecules, cells, or organisms autonomously come together to form complex structures or systems.

Self-assembly is a promising paradigm in additive manufacturing that leverages the principles of bio mimicry to create materials and structures with minimal external intervention. It offers several advantages, including reduced production costs, increased efficiency, and the potential for highly customized, intricate designs. Here, we delve into the world of bio-inspired additive manufacturing techniques with a focus on self-assembly.

1. Biological Inspiration:

The natural world is a treasure trove of inspiration for self-assembly techniques in 3D printing. From the self-assembly of proteins into intricate functional structures to the remarkable formation of complex biological tissues, the efficiency and precision of nature's self-organizing processes have captivated researchers. Biomimetic 3D printing aims to harness these processes to create innovative, sustainable, and cost-effective manufacturing methods.

2. Principles of Self-Assembly:

Self-assembly in 3D printing relies on the intrinsic properties of materials and their interactions. It typically involves the design of materials with specific shapes, properties, or chemical compositions that enable them to spontaneously arrange into desired structures. These materials may include shape-memory polymers, responsive nanoparticles, or even bioengineered cells that can grow and assemble into intricate patterns.

3. Applications:

Bio-inspired additive manufacturing techniques with a focus on self-assembly have a wide range of potential applications. Some notable examples include:

Medical Implants: Researchers are exploring self-assembling materials for creating customized medical implants. These materials could adapt to the patient's anatomy, promoting better integration and reduced risk of rejection.

Aerospace: Self-assembling materials and structures could lead to lightweight, complex components for aerospace applications. These structures could adapt to changing conditions and repair themselves, reducing maintenance costs.

Construction: Self-assembling building materials, such as bricks that arrange themselves into specific patterns, could revolutionize construction, making it more efficient and sustainable.

Electronics: Self-assembling electronic components could lead to faster and more precise manufacturing processes, improving the performance of devices.

4. Challenges and Future Directions:

While the potential of self-assembly in bio-inspired additive manufacturing is promising, there are several challenges to overcome. These include the need for precise control over self-assembly processes, ensuring the materials used are both safe and sustainable, and addressing scalability issues for mass production.

The future of self-assembly in 3D printing lies in interdisciplinary research, where materials science, biology, and engineering converge. By drawing inspiration from nature and understanding its self-organizing principles, scientists and engineers can continue to push the boundaries of what is possible in additive manufacturing. With on-going innovation, bio-inspired additive manufacturing techniques, particularly those based on self-assembly, are poised to revolutionize a wide array of industries, offering sustainable, efficient, and highly customizable solutions for the challenges of the future.

CHAPTER TWO

BIO MATERIALS AND BIO HEALTHCARE DESIGN

Biomaterials, Design of Forms- (Hexagonal unit cells, intrinsic disorder, anisotropy), Design of materials- (Hierarchy, fracture tough materials, structural colours, Actuating Materials, Bio-Compatible Materials). Bio-Mechanics, Applications of Biomaterials and Bio systems in Health care design (Human Prosthetics, Parasitic Wasp-Inspired Needle, Octopus-Inspired Sucker for Tissue Grafting, Peacock-Inspired Biosensors, Gecko-Inspired Surgical Glue) Robotics, Marine and Aeronautical.

Biomaterials

Biomaterials are a class of materials that have garnered significant attention and application across various fields, particularly in medicine and biotechnology. These materials are specifically designed to interact with biological systems, such as the human body, in a way that is safe and effective. The term "biomaterials" encompasses a wide range of substances, including synthetic polymers, metals, ceramics, and natural materials.

One of the primary objectives of biomaterials is to enhance the interaction between the material and the biological environment in which it is used. This often involves tailoring the physical, chemical, and mechanical properties of the material to suit a particular application. Biomaterials are used in a variety of medical devices, such as artificial joints, dental implants, and cardiovascular stents, as well as in tissue engineering and drug delivery systems.

The development of biomaterials is a multidisciplinary field that draws from materials science, chemistry, biology, and engineering. Researchers in this field work to create materials that are biocompatible, meaning they do not elicit harmful immune responses or toxic reactions when they come into contact with living tissues. Additionally, biomaterials must be durable, providing long-term functionality, and they should be able to integrate with the body's natural processes, such as tissue regeneration.

The choice of biomaterial for a particular application depends on a variety of factors, including the intended use, the properties of the material, and the specific biological environment it will encounter. For example, metals like titanium are commonly used in orthopaedic implants due to their strength and biocompatibility, while biodegradable polymers are employed in drug delivery systems because they can slowly release drugs into the body.

Biomaterials research continues to advance, with on-going efforts to improve the performance and safety of these materials. This involves innovations in material design, surface modification, and the development of new biomaterials with enhanced properties. The goal is to create biomaterials that can better mimic the natural properties of living tissues, thereby improving patient outcomes and overall quality of life.

Biomaterials play a crucial role in modern medicine and biotechnology by providing materials that can interact with the human body in a safe and effective manner. This field is continually evolving, with researchers striving to develop biomaterials that are more biocompatible, durable, and capable of integrating seamlessly with biological systems, ultimately improving the success and longevity of medical treatments and devices.

Design of Forms- (Hexagonal unit cells)

Design of forms using hexagonal unit cells is a concept that finds its application in various fields, including architecture, crystallography, and materials science. Hexagonal unit cells provide unique geometric characteristics and aesthetic possibilities that differentiate them from other unit cell shapes, such as cubic or tetragonal cells.

In architecture, the use of hexagonal unit cells can lead to distinctive and visually appealing structures. The hexagonal shape offers a balanced blend of symmetry and uniqueness, making it suitable for both practical and artistic purposes. Architects often incorporate hexagonal patterns into building facades, interior design, and structural components, creating visually engaging and structurally sound spaces.

In crystallography, the hexagonal unit cell is an essential concept for understanding the arrangement of atoms in certain crystalline structures. Materials with hexagonal unit cells exhibit unique properties and symmetries. The hexagonal lattice is particularly relevant in the study of minerals and some metals. It provides a framework for describing the arrangement of atoms or ions in these materials, helping researchers predict their physical and chemical properties.

The hexagonal unit cell is also vital in materials science, especially in the design of advanced materials. Hexagonal structures can offer benefits in terms of mechanical strength, thermal conductivity, and electrical properties. By manipulating the arrangement of atoms within hexagonal unit cells, engineers and scientists can create innovative materials with tailored properties for specific applications.

Additionally, hexagonal unit cells are known for their close-packing arrangement of spheres, which maximizes the space-filling efficiency. This property is exploited in various fields, such as packing optimization algorithms, where hexagonal unit cells can be used to efficiently fill space while minimizing voids, which is particularly important in packing and stacking problems.

The design of forms using hexagonal unit cells has a broad range of applications in architecture, crystallography, and materials science. The unique geometric properties and structural characteristics of hexagonal unit cells make them a valuable tool for creating aesthetically pleasing designs and understanding the arrangement of atoms in various materials. Whether in the construction of innovative buildings, the study of crystal structures, or the development of advanced materials, the hexagonal unit cell offers endless opportunities for creative and functional design.

Design of Forms- (Intrinsic disorder)

Designing forms with consideration for intrinsic disorder is an essential aspect of creating user-friendly and effective interfaces. Intrinsic disorder, in this context, refers to the variability and unpredictability of user behaviour and input when interacting with forms and applications. Designing forms that account for this disorder can significantly improve the user experience and increase the chances of obtaining accurate and valuable data.

Flexibility and Adaptability: One of the primary principles in designing forms to accommodate intrinsic disorder is flexibility. Forms should be adaptable to various input styles, devices, and screen sizes. Users might access the form on different platforms, from mobile phones to desktop computers, so ensuring that the form can adjust to different screen sizes is crucial.

Progressive Disclosure: To manage complexity and avoid overwhelming users, consider using progressive disclosure. Start with a minimal set of required fields and provide options for additional information. This approach allows users to focus on the essentials and provides a sense of control, reducing the disorder that can arise from overwhelming forms.

Clear Instructions and Validation: Provide clear and concise instructions for each form field. Users should have a good understanding of what is expected in each input field. Validation should also be immediate and helpful. When users make mistakes, error messages should be informative and guide them towards correction. This approach minimizes user frustration and errors due to disorderly input.

Auto fill and Autocomplete: Use auto fill and autocomplete suggestions to help users with commonly entered data. This feature reduces the likelihood of user errors and speeds up the form-filling process. This is particularly useful for long forms or forms with numerous repetitive fields.

Conditional Logic: Incorporate conditional logic to show or hide form fields based on previous responses. This reduces clutter and guides users through the form logically. Users who encounter forms that are not relevant to their needs may become frustrated, leading to abandonment.

Testing and Feedback: Extensive user testing is crucial to identify disorderly behaviours and areas where users struggle. Gathering user feedback can provide insights into the specific issues that need to be addressed in the form design. Continuous improvement based on user feedback is a key strategy to minimize disorder in form interactions.

Accessibility: Ensure that your forms are accessible to all users, including those with disabilities. This means providing support for screen readers, keyboard navigation, and other assistive technologies. Accessibility features can help users with various disorders effectively interact with the form.

Mobile Optimization: With the increasing use of mobile devices, optimizing forms for mobile users is critical. Designing forms that are touch-friendly, with appropriately sized input fields and buttons, can help minimize disorder when users interact with forms on smaller screens.

Aesthetic and Functional Consistency: Consistency in design elements, such as fonts, colours, and button placements, contributes to a more intuitive and less disorderly user experience. When users encounter a familiar interface, they are less likely to make errors or become disoriented.

Error Recovery: In case of errors or incomplete submissions, provide a straightforward path for users to correct their mistakes or continue where they left off. Disorder can arise when users don't know how to recover from errors or navigate back to the form.

Designing forms with intrinsic disorder in mind is essential for creating user-friendly interfaces. By considering flexibility, clear instructions, adaptive features, and user feedback, you can reduce the disorder that users may experience while interacting with forms. A well-designed form not only improves the user experience but also results in more accurate and valuable data collection.

<u>Design of Forms- (anisotropy)</u>

Designing forms with consideration for anisotropy is an important aspect of various engineering and material science applications. Anisotropy refers to the directional dependence of a material's properties, where these properties vary with respect to the direction in which they are measured. It is a key factor to consider when designing forms, especially in fields such as material engineering, geology, and architecture.

When designing forms with anisotropy in mind, several critical considerations come into play:

Material Selection: The choice of materials is crucial when dealing with anisotropy. Different materials exhibit varying degrees of anisotropy. For instance, wood, composite materials, and many crystals are highly anisotropic, while metals tend to be more isotropic. Selecting a material with the appropriate anisotropic characteristics is essential for achieving the desired form and function.

Directional Properties: Understanding how the material's properties change with respect to direction is essential. For instance, the stiffness, thermal conductivity, electrical conductivity, and mechanical strength of a material can differ significantly along different axes. Designers need to consider these directional properties to ensure that the form they create meets the specific requirements of the application.

Structural Integrity: When designing forms with anisotropic materials, maintaining structural integrity is a challenge. Engineers and designers must consider load-bearing requirements and the direction of applied forces to ensure that the form can withstand these forces without deformation or failure.

Manufacturing Techniques: The manufacturing process must also be considered in the design of anisotropic forms. Some manufacturing methods, such as 3D printing, can allow for precise control over material deposition in multiple directions, enabling the creation of forms with tailored anisotropic properties.

Cost and Efficiency: Depending on the material and design, achieving anisotropic forms can be costly. It's crucial to strike a balance between the desired form and the practicality of manufacturing while considering cost-effectiveness.

Optimization: The design process may involve optimization algorithms to determine the ideal form that maximizes the benefits of anisotropy. This could involve adjusting the shape and orientation of components to align with the material's anisotropic properties.

Real-world Applications: Anisotropic forms are used in various applications. In civil engineering, the design of structures like bridges or skyscrapers may involve considering the anisotropic properties of materials. In geology, understanding the anisotropy of rock formations is critical for excavation and tunnelling projects.

Designing forms with anisotropy in mind requires a deep understanding of material properties, structural engineering, and manufacturing processes. By taking these factors into account, designers and engineers can create forms that exploit anisotropic characteristics to achieve superior performance and functionality in various real-world applications.

Design of materials- (Hierarchy).

Design of materials involves a multifaceted approach to creating substances with specific properties and functionalities. This process can be described in terms of a hierarchy, which encompasses various levels of design and control. The hierarchy of materials design typically consists of four main levels:

Atomic and Molecular Level:

At the most fundamental level, materials design starts with the manipulation and control of atoms and molecules. Researchers and scientists strive to understand the structure and behaviour of individual atoms and molecules. This knowledge is essential for tailoring the properties of materials at higher levels. Techniques like molecular modelling and quantum chemistry are employed to predict how atoms and molecules interact to form desired structures.

Nanostructure Level:

Building upon the atomic and molecular understanding, materials designers work at the nanostructure level. This involves arranging atoms and molecules into specific patterns to create nanomaterial's with unique properties. Nanotechnology plays a crucial role in engineering materials at this scale. Researchers work with techniques such as nanolithography, chemical synthesis, and self-assembly to create nanomaterial's like quantum dots, carbon nanotubes, and nonporous materials.

Microstructure Level:

Moving up the hierarchy, materials are designed at the microstructure level. This level involves manipulating the arrangement of nanoscale components to create macro scale structures. For instance, controlling the grain size and orientation in metals can significantly affect their mechanical properties. Material designers use processes such as alloying, heat treatment, and surface coatings to customize the microstructure for specific applications.

Macro scale Level:

Finally, at the macro scale level, materials are designed for specific applications and end-users. This is where the properties and functionalities of materials are tailored to meet the requirements of a particular product or system. Engineers and designers select the appropriate materials from the previous levels and combine them into a final product. This may involve shaping, joining, and assembling materials to achieve the desired mechanical, thermal, electrical, or optical properties.

The hierarchy in materials design is interconnected, with each level building upon the knowledge and control gained from the level below. Successful materials design requires a deep understanding of the properties and behaviour of materials at each level and the ability to manipulate them for desired outcomes. By designing materials with precision at all these levels, scientists and engineers can develop innovative materials that find applications in fields ranging from electronics and aerospace to medicine and sustainable energy.

Design of materials- (fracture tough materials).

Designing materials with high fracture toughness is essential in various industries, including aerospace, automotive, construction, and medical devices. Fracture toughness refers to a material's ability to resist crack propagation and withstand external loads without catastrophic failure. Achieving high fracture toughness involves a complex interplay of material selection, microstructure design, and processing techniques.

Material Selection:

Choosing the right material is the first step in designing high fracture toughness materials. Engineers often opt for tough materials like metals, polymers, ceramics, and composites, depending on the specific application. For example, steel is renowned for its high fracture toughness, making it suitable for structural components in buildings and bridges. Polymers are chosen for their flexibility and impact resistance, while ceramics offer excellent resistance to thermal and chemical damage.

Microstructure Design:

The microstructure of a material plays a critical role in its fracture toughness. Controlling the arrangement of atoms, grains, phases, and defects within the material can enhance its toughness. Some key strategies include:

Grain size control: Fine-grained materials often exhibit higher toughness due to increased resistance to crack propagation. Grain boundaries can act as barriers to crack growth.

Phase transformations: Certain materials can be engineered to undergo phase transformations under stress, absorbing energy and preventing catastrophic failure.

Inclusion and reinforcement: Adding micro-scale inclusions or reinforcements can toughen a material. For example, carbon fibres in a polymer matrix can significantly enhance fracture toughness.

Residual stresses: Inducing controlled residual stresses can mitigate crack initiation and propagation.

Processing Techniques:

The manufacturing process significantly affects the fracture toughness of materials. Heat treatment, alloying, and various processing techniques can be used to enhance toughness. For instance, tempering steel involves controlled heating and cooling to modify its microstructure, improving toughness. In the case of polymers, blending with impact modifiers can increase toughness.

Testing and Analysis:

Characterizing the fracture toughness of a material is essential for quality control and design optimization. Common tests include Charpy and Izod impact tests for polymers, and the KIc and J-integral tests for metals. These tests help assess a material's ability to absorb energy and resist crack propagation.

Composite Materials:

Composite materials, which combine different constituents, can be tailored to achieve high fracture toughness. For instance, laminated composites, like carbon-fibre-reinforced composites, offer a balance between strength and toughness due to the arrangement of different materials in distinct layers.

Simulation and Modelling:

Advanced computational tools and modelling techniques are employed to predict and optimize fracture toughness. Finite element analysis and molecular dynamics simulations can help engineers understand how materials will behave under different loads and conditions.

The design of materials with high fracture toughness is a multidisciplinary endeavour that involves material selection, microstructure design, processing techniques, testing, and analysis. It is a critical aspect of ensuring the safety and durability of various structures and components in engineering applications. Achieving high fracture toughness often requires a deep understanding of material science, advanced manufacturing processes, and the integration of computational tools for optimization.

<u>Design of materials- (structural colours).</u>

Structural colours are a fascinating phenomenon in the field of materials science and design. Unlike pigments, which achieve their colours through the selective absorption and reflection of specific wavelengths of light, structural colours are generated through the interaction of light with the microstructure of a material. This unique characteristic has intrigued scientists and designers alike, as it opens up new possibilities for creating vibrant, dynamic, and iridescent colours without the use of dyes or pigments.

The basis of structural colours lies in the interaction of light with intricate nanostructures or microstructures within the material. These structures are typically on the scale of the wavelength of visible light, which ranges from 400 to 700 nanometres. When light encounters these structures, it undergoes various optical effects, including interference, diffraction, and scattering, which result in the generation of colours.

One of the most well-known examples of structural colours in nature is the brilliant hues seen on the wings of butterflies, the feathers of peacocks, and the shells of certain beetles. These vibrant colours are not produced by pigments but rather by microscopic structures that manipulate the incident light. These structures can be lattices, layers, or even tiny holes in the material, which cause constructive interference for specific wavelengths of light. The result is a stunning array of colours that shift with the viewing angle and lighting conditions.

In the realm of materials design, researchers have sought to replicate and harness the principles behind structural colours. This has led to the development of photonic crystals, met materials, and nanostructured coatings, which can be tailored to produce specific colours or optical effects. These materials find applications in various industries, including textiles, cosmetics, and displays. For instance, researchers have designed fabrics that change colour with stretching or folding, or cosmetics that exhibit different hues under varying lighting conditions.

Structural colours also offer eco-friendly alternatives to traditional coloration methods. By eliminating the need for toxic dyes and pigments, materials designed with structural colours can contribute to sustainability and reduce the environmental impact of the fashion and textile industries. Additionally, these materials hold promise in fields like anti-counterfeiting technology, as their intricate and difficult-to-replicate structures can serve as security features on documents or products.

Moreover, the potential applications of structural colours are not limited to aesthetics alone. In the realm of photonics, these materials can be integrated into optical devices and sensors to manipulate light and create tuneable filters or displays. Their ability to change colour or optical properties in response to external stimuli, such as temperature or humidity, can be leveraged for sensing applications.

The design of materials with structural colours represents a captivating intersection of science and art. It offers a unique approach to achieving vibrant and dynamic colours by harnessing the intricate interplay of light and nanostructures. The applications of structural colours are broad, spanning from fashion and cosmetics to advanced technologies, and their eco-friendly nature adds a layer of sustainability to the mix. As our understanding of these materials continues to evolve, we can expect to see even more innovative and creative uses emerging in the world of design and beyond.

<u>Design of materials- (Actuating Materials).</u>

Design of materials for actuating applications is a multifaceted field that plays a pivotal role in the development of various innovative technologies and devices. Actuating materials are specifically engineered to change their shape, size, or properties in response to external stimuli, such as electrical, thermal, magnetic, or chemical inputs. These materials find applications in diverse areas, including robotics, aerospace, medical devices, and consumer electronics. The design of actuating materials involves careful consideration of their composition, structure, and functional properties to achieve desired performance characteristics.

One of the primary challenges in designing actuating materials is selecting the appropriate type of material that can exhibit the desired actuation behaviour. Some common classes of actuating materials include shape memory alloys, piezoelectric materials, electro active polymers, and magnetic shape memory alloys. Each class has its unique set of properties and capabilities, making it essential to choose the material that best aligns with the application's requirements.

The composition of actuating materials is critical in determining their responsiveness to external stimuli. For instance, shape memory alloys are composed of metals like nickel and titanium, which exhibit the ability to revert to a predetermined shape after being deformed when subjected to heat or stress. The composition and phase transformation behaviour of these alloys must be precisely engineered to achieve the desired actuation performance.

Furthermore, the microstructure and crystallographic features of actuating materials play a crucial role in defining their actuation characteristics. Researchers often employ advanced manufacturing techniques, such as additive manufacturing or controlled alloying, to tailor the microstructure of materials for enhanced actuation. The design of microstructures that enable reversible and controlled deformation is a fundamental aspect of actuating material development.

Another key aspect in actuating material design is the control of external stimuli. For example, in the case of piezoelectric materials, applying an electrical voltage leads to mechanical deformation, and the precise control of voltage allows for fine-tuning the actuation response. Designing control systems and interfaces that enable the precise manipulation of these stimuli is integral to the successful implementation of actuating materials in practical applications.

Environmental considerations are also essential in actuating material design. Some actuating materials may be sensitive to factors like temperature, humidity, or chemical exposure. Therefore, encapsulation and protective coatings are often incorporated to enhance their durability and stability in various operating conditions.

In addition to the technical aspects, ethical and safety considerations are paramount in the design of actuating materials. Ensuring that actuating materials are safe for use in medical devices or consumer products, for example, requires rigorous testing and compliance with regulatory standards.

The design of actuating materials is a complex and interdisciplinary field that brings together principles from materials science, engineering, and physics. It involves careful selection of materials, precise control of composition and microstructure, and the development of control systems to achieve the desired actuation behaviour. Furthermore, addressing environmental, ethical, and safety concerns is vital for the successful integration of actuating materials into real-world applications. As technology continues to advance, actuating materials will likely play an increasingly significant role in shaping the future of various industries.

Design of materials- (Bio-Compatible Materials).

Designing bio-compatible materials is a crucial area of research and development in the field of materials science and engineering. Bio-compatible materials are substances that interact harmoniously with living organisms without causing harm, rejection, or adverse reactions. They play a pivotal role in various medical and biological applications, including medical implants, drug delivery systems, tissue engineering, and more. Designing these materials requires a deep understanding of both the biological systems they will interact with and the physical and chemical properties of the materials themselves.

Key considerations in the design of bio-compatible materials include:

Biocompatibility: The primary objective of bio-compatible materials is to ensure they do not elicit harmful responses from the body. This involves assessing how the material interacts with cells, tissues, and the immune system. Factors such as cytotoxicity, immunogenicity, and inflammation need to be minimized to ensure the material's biocompatibility.

Material Selection: The choice of material is critical. Common bio-compatible materials include biodegradable polymers, ceramics, metals, and composites. The selection depends on the specific application and the intended duration of interaction with biological systems. For example, biodegradable polymers are suitable for drug delivery systems, while titanium alloys are often used in orthopaedic implants.

Surface Modifications: Surface properties of materials play a significant role in their interaction with biological entities. Techniques like surface functionalization, coating, and texturing can be employed to enhance cell adhesion, reduce inflammation, and improve the overall biocompatibility of the material.

Mechanical Compatibility: In applications such as orthopaedic implants, it is essential that bio-compatible materials possess mechanical properties similar to the tissues they are replacing. This ensures that the implants can withstand the mechanical stresses within the body without causing damage.

Degradation and Biodegradability: For temporary implants and drug delivery systems, the rate of material degradation is a crucial factor. The design should consider how the material breaks down over time and whether the degradation by-products are safe for the body.

Drug Release Profiles: In drug delivery systems, the design must control the release of therapeutic agents at a predetermined rate. This requires the incorporation of drug carriers, Nano carriers, or polymers that can release drugs in a controlled and sustained manner.

Regulatory Compliance: Bio-compatible materials need to meet stringent regulatory requirements to ensure they are safe for use in clinical settings. These materials must undergo thorough testing and validation to demonstrate their safety and efficacy.

Long-Term Stability: For permanent implants, the materials must maintain their properties and integrity over extended periods in the body. This involves designing materials that are resistant to corrosion, wear, and fatigue.

Bio integration: To facilitate the integration of bio-compatible materials with surrounding tissues, the design should promote tissue regeneration and remodelling around the implant. This can involve incorporating bioactive components or structures that promote cell adhesion and growth.

The design of bio-compatible materials is a complex and multidisciplinary field that draws from materials science, biology, chemistry, and engineering. Researchers in this field aim to create materials that not only perform their intended function but also do so without causing harm to the host organism. Advances in bio-compatible materials have revolutionized medical treatments, enabling safer and more effective solutions for a wide range of health conditions.

Bio-Mechanics

Biomechanics is the interdisciplinary field that combines principles of biology and mechanics to understand the mechanical aspects of living organisms. It explores how biological systems, ranging from cells and tissues to entire organisms, interact with and respond to mechanical forces. Biomechanics plays a crucial role in various fields, including sports science, medicine, engineering, and biology.

One of the key aspects of biomechanics is the study of movement. Researchers in this field examine how muscles, bones, and joints work together to produce motion. This is particularly important in sports science, where biomechanical analysis helps athletes and coaches improve performance and reduce the risk of injuries. Biomechanical principles are used to design sports equipment, such as running shoes, to enhance athletic performance.

In medicine, biomechanics is essential for understanding the mechanics of the human body, which can aid in diagnosing and treating various medical conditions. Orthopaedic surgeons, for example, use biomechanical principles to analyse and correct issues related to the musculoskeletal system, such as fractures, joint problems, and spinal deformities. Biomechanics also plays a role in designing prosthetic devices and orthotic braces, which can greatly improve the quality of life for individuals with physical disabilities.

Biomechanics is not limited to the macroscopic scale of human movement. It also encompasses the study of cellular biomechanics, where researchers investigate how cells respond to mechanical forces and how these forces influence cell behaviour. Understanding cellular biomechanics is vital in fields like tissue engineering, where researchers aim to create functional tissues for transplantation or regenerative medicine.

Furthermore, biomechanics contributes to the understanding of the mechanics of various organisms and their adaptations to different environments. For instance, studying the biomechanics of bird flight can help researchers design more efficient aircraft, and analysing the biomechanics of fish swimming can inform the development of underwater robotics.

Biomechanics is a multidisciplinary field that bridges biology and mechanics to unravel the mechanical intricacies of living organisms. Its applications are wide-ranging, impacting sports, medicine, engineering, and biology. By delving into the biomechanical principles governing the form and function of living systems, researchers and practitioners can advance our knowledge of the natural world and improve human health and performance.

Applications of Biomaterials and Bio systems in Health care design (Human Prosthetics)

The field of healthcare design has seen remarkable advancements with the integration of biomaterials and bio systems, particularly in the development of human prosthetics. Prosthetic devices have evolved from rudimentary, function-focused designs to highly sophisticated and anatomically accurate solutions, thanks to the incorporation of cutting-edge biomaterials and bio systems. This essay explores the profound impact of biomaterials and bio systems on the design of human prosthetics and their significant contributions to improving the quality of life for individuals with limb loss.

Biomaterials in Prosthetic Design

Biomaterials are synthetic or natural materials that interact with biological systems, often to replace or augment bodily functions. When it comes to human prosthetics, the choice of biomaterials plays a pivotal role in the design and performance of the device. Some key applications of biomaterials in prosthetic design include:

a. Biocompatibility: Biomaterials are selected for their ability to integrate with the human body without causing adverse reactions. This is crucial for ensuring that prosthetic devices are well-tolerated by the user, minimizing the risk of infections or tissue rejection.

b. Strength and Durability: Prosthetic limbs need to withstand significant forces and wear and tear. Biomaterials are chosen for their mechanical strength, ensuring that the prosthetic can handle daily activities and various physical stresses.

c. Lightweight Design: Modern prosthetics are designed to be lightweight, mimicking the weight and feel of natural limbs. Biomaterials help achieve this by providing strength without unnecessary weight, enhancing the user's comfort and mobility.

d. Customizability: Some biomaterials can be 3D printed or moulded to create custom-fit prosthetic components, enabling a more precise fit and improved comfort for the wearer.

Bio Systems in Prosthetic Design

Bio systems, which often include advanced sensors and control mechanisms, have revolutionized prosthetic design by enabling greater functionality and a more intuitive user experience. The integration of bio systems allows prosthetic devices to respond more naturally to the user's movements and sensory input. Key applications of bio systems in prosthetic design include:

a. Myoelectric Prosthetics: Myoelectric prosthetics use bio systems to detect electrical signals generated by the user's muscles. By interpreting these signals, the prosthetic limb can be controlled with precision, allowing users to perform fine motor tasks, such as grasping and manipulating objects.

b. Sensory Feedback: Bio systems can incorporate sensory feedback mechanisms that provide users with information about pressure, temperature, and texture, enhancing their ability to interact with the environment.

c. Machine Learning and AI: The integration of machine learning and artificial intelligence allows prosthetic limbs to adapt and learn from the user's movements, making them more responsive and user-friendly over time.

d. Telemetry and Remote Monitoring: Bio systems can transmit data to healthcare providers, allowing for remote monitoring and adjustments to the prosthetic's settings, thereby optimizing its performance.

Advantages and Impact on Healthcare

The integration of biomaterials and bio systems in healthcare design, particularly in prosthetic devices, has brought several advantages and a transformative impact:

a. Improved Functionality: Prosthetic limbs with advanced biomaterials and bio systems provide users with enhanced functionality, allowing them to engage in a wider range of activities, leading to an improved quality of life.

b. Psychological Well-being: The anatomical accuracy, customizability, and sensory feedback provided by these prosthetic devices have a positive impact on the user's psychological well-being, reducing the stigma associated with limb loss.

c. Longevity and Maintenance: Biomaterials and bio systems have led to prosthetic devices that are more durable and easier to maintain, reducing the frequency of replacements and costs associated with prosthetic care.

d. Enhanced Research Opportunities: The development of biomaterials and bio systems for prosthetic design has paved the way for further research and innovation in the fields of materials science, engineering, and biotechnology, with potential applications beyond prosthetics.

The integration of biomaterials and bio systems in healthcare design has revolutionized the field of human prosthetics, leading to more functional, comfortable, and natural-looking solutions for individuals with limb loss. The use of biocompatible materials, coupled with advanced sensing and control mechanisms, has not only improved the physical capabilities of prosthetic limbs but has also positively influenced the psychological and emotional well-being of users. As technology continues to advance, the future of human prosthetics holds the promise of even more sophisticated and life-changing innovations.

<u>Applications of Biomaterials and Bio systems in Health care design (Parasitic Wasp-Inspired Needle)</u>

Biomaterials and bio systems have found extensive applications in healthcare design, and one innovative example of this is the development of a parasitic wasp-inspired needle. This bio-inspired approach leverages the remarkable adaptations and mechanisms found in nature to create solutions that address specific challenges in healthcare.

Precision Targeting: The parasitic wasp-inspired needle is designed to mimic the ovipositor of parasitic wasps. These insects have evolved an incredibly precise and efficient way to deposit their eggs within a host organism. By emulating the structure and mechanics of the wasp's ovipositor, scientists and engineers have created a needle capable of accurately delivering medications or treatments to precise locations within the human body. This level of precision is particularly valuable in applications such as tumour targeting, where medications can be delivered directly to cancer cells, minimizing damage to healthy tissue.

Minimized Tissue Damage: The needle design also helps in minimizing tissue damage during insertion. Traditional needles can cause trauma and inflammation at the injection site, but the parasitic wasp-inspired needle's fine, serrated tip allows for smoother penetration, reducing pain and discomfort for the patient.

Drug Delivery: Biomaterials play a critical role in the construction of these needles. Biocompatible materials are used to ensure that the needle does not provoke an immune response or adverse reactions in the body. Additionally, the needle's size and shape can be tailored to accommodate various drug formulations, enabling controlled release and targeted drug delivery.

Minimally Invasive Surgery: The design of the parasitic wasp-inspired needle can also be applied to minimally invasive surgical procedures. Surgeons can use these needles to access hard-to-reach areas of the body with minimal damage to surrounding tissues. This is especially important in delicate procedures such as neurosurgery.

Endoscopy and Biopsy: In endoscopy and biopsy applications, these needles allow for more precise and less invasive tissue sampling. The fine, flexible structure of the needle makes it ideal for collecting small tissue samples or obtaining diagnostic specimens.

Reduced Patient Discomfort: Due to their fine and precise nature, parasitic wasp-inspired needles reduce patient discomfort during procedures, making it easier for individuals to tolerate medical interventions and improving patient compliance.

Lower Risk of Infection: The materials used in these needles can also incorporate antimicrobial properties, further reducing the risk of infection associated with invasive medical procedures.

Customization: One of the advantages of biomaterials is their flexibility and adaptability. Engineers can customize the properties of these needles to suit specific healthcare needs, such as varying sizes, flexibility, and even surface coatings for specific drug delivery requirements.

Sustainability: Biomaterials used in these needles can be sourced from renewable and eco-friendly materials, contributing to sustainability efforts in healthcare design.

The parasitic wasp-inspired needle is a prime example of how biomaterials and bio systems have revolutionized healthcare design. By emulating nature's efficient mechanisms, these needles offer precision, reduced tissue damage, and improved patient comfort, making them valuable tools in drug delivery, minimally invasive surgery, endoscopy, and other medical procedures. Their potential for customization and sustainable design further underscores their importance in advancing healthcare technologies.

Applications of Biomaterials and Bio systems in Health care design (Octopus-Inspired Sucker for Tissue Grafting)

The field of healthcare design has witnessed remarkable advancements through the incorporation of biomaterials and bio-inspired systems. One such innovation involves the development of octopus-inspired suckers for tissue grafting, which is a promising application of biomaterials and bio systems in healthcare.

Biomaterials, by definition, are materials that interact with biological systems to enhance or restore the function of living tissues. They can be synthetic or natural, and their design plays a critical role in the success of various medical procedures. Octopus-inspired suckers, which draw inspiration from the remarkable adhesive capabilities of octopus tentacles, represent a novel approach to tissue grafting in healthcare design.

Here are some key aspects of this innovative application:

Adhesion and Tissue Integration:

Octopuses are known for their exceptional ability to adhere to various surfaces, including irregular and wet substrates. This unique capability has led to the development of specialized biomaterials and suction systems that mimic the structure and function of octopus suckers. These materials can be used in healthcare for secure adhesion of graft tissues to host tissues, thereby promoting better integration and healing.

Minimally Invasive Procedures:

The octopus-inspired sucker technology can enable minimally invasive surgical procedures. By using these biomaterials, healthcare professionals can attach graft tissues without the need for extensive incisions, reducing patient discomfort, postoperative recovery times, and the risk of complications.

Reduced Foreign Body Response:

One of the challenges in tissue grafting is the host's immune response to foreign materials. Biomaterials inspired by octopus suckers can be designed to minimize the host's immune reaction, making it possible to graft tissues without excessive inflammation or rejection.

Improved Wound Healing:

The adhesion and integration properties of octopus-inspired suckers can accelerate wound healing and reduce scarring. By enhancing tissue grafting techniques, patients can experience faster recovery and improved outcomes.

Enhanced Precision:

Bio-inspired systems like octopus-inspired suckers can provide healthcare professionals with greater control and precision during surgical procedures. This can result in more accurate tissue placement, which is particularly crucial in delicate operations such as organ transplantation.

Versatility and Multidisciplinary Collaboration:

The development of octopus-inspired suckers involves a multidisciplinary approach that combines materials science, biomechanics, and medical expertise. Such collaborations open up new avenues for innovation in healthcare design, allowing for the creation of advanced surgical tools and materials that can be customized to specific patient needs.

The use of biomaterials and bio-inspired systems, such as octopus-inspired suckers, in healthcare design represents a significant advancement in the field of tissue grafting and surgery. These innovative materials and technologies hold the potential to revolutionize surgical procedures, making them less invasive, more precise, and with improved patient outcomes. The integration of biomaterials and bio systems in healthcare continues to open doors for ground breaking solutions and improvements in patient care.

<u>**Applications of Biomaterials and Bio systems in Health care design (Peacock-Inspired Biosensors)**</u>

Biomaterials and bio systems have revolutionized healthcare design by providing innovative solutions for diagnosis, monitoring, and treatment. One intriguing development in this field is the emergence of peacock-inspired biosensors, which draw inspiration from the vibrant colors of peacock feathers. These biosensors integrate biomaterials and bio-inspired design principles to create advanced diagnostic tools that offer enhanced sensitivity, specificity, and versatility in healthcare applications.

The Inspiration from Peacock Feathers:

Peacock feathers are renowned for their iridescent colours, which result from the unique microscopic structure of the feather barbules. These structural colours are produced by the interference and scattering of light due to the periodic arrangement of nanostructures. This principle has been applied to the development of biosensors, where the biomaterials mimic the nanostructures found in peacock feathers to enable precise detection and monitoring of various biomolecules.

Applications of Peacock-Inspired Biosensors in Healthcare Design:

Disease Diagnosis:

Peacock-inspired biosensors are particularly valuable for early disease diagnosis. By utilizing the nanostructures reminiscent of peacock feathers, these biosensors can detect specific biomarkers in bodily fluids, such as blood or urine, with exceptional sensitivity. This is critical for diagnosing conditions like cancer, diabetes, and infectious diseases at an early stage, increasing the chances of successful treatment.

Monitoring of Chronic Conditions:

Chronic diseases like diabetes and cardiovascular disorders require continuous monitoring. Peacock-inspired biosensors can be integrated into wearable devices or implantable systems to provide real-time monitoring of relevant biomarkers. These biosensors can offer patients and healthcare professionals valuable insights into disease management and help prevent complications.

Drug Development and Pharmacology:

In drug development, peacock-inspired biosensors play a pivotal role. They enable researchers to assess the effectiveness of potential drug compounds by monitoring their interactions with specific target molecules. This information can expedite the drug discovery process and lead to the development of more efficient and safer pharmaceuticals.

Environmental Sensing:

Beyond clinical applications, these biosensors can be employed in environmental sensing. They can detect contaminants, pollutants, and toxins in air, water, and soil. By offering a quick and reliable means of assessing environmental quality, they contribute to public health and the preservation of ecosystems.

Point-of-Care Testing:

Peacock-inspired biosensors are well-suited for point-of-care testing. They can be integrated into compact, portable devices that allow rapid and on-site analysis of various biomolecules. This is especially valuable in remote or resource-limited settings, where access to advanced laboratory facilities may be limited.

Challenges and Future Directions:

While peacock-inspired biosensors hold great promise, several challenges must be addressed. These include optimizing the biomaterials used in these sensors, ensuring their long-term stability, and refining their specificity and selectivity for different biomolecules. Additionally, the integration of these biosensors into practical healthcare systems and ensuring regulatory compliance are important considerations for the future.

The application of biomaterials and bio-inspired design principles in healthcare design, particularly in the development of peacock-inspired biosensors, offers a new dimension to diagnostic and monitoring tools. These biosensors, inspired by the natural world, have the potential to significantly enhance healthcare outcomes by enabling early disease diagnosis, precise monitoring, and advancing drug development. As technology continues to evolve, the impact of peacock-inspired biosensors on healthcare design is expected to grow, further improving patient care and our understanding of the biological world.

Applications of Biomaterials and Bio systems in Health care design (Gecko-Inspired Surgical Glue)

Applications of biomaterials and bio systems in healthcare design have made significant strides in improving patient outcomes and enhancing medical procedures. One innovative example is the development of gecko-inspired surgical glue, which draws inspiration from nature to address the challenges of tissue adhesion in medical settings.

Geckos are known for their remarkable ability to climb walls and ceilings, thanks to the intricate structures on their feet. These structures include millions of tiny hair-like projections called setae, each tipped with even smaller structures known as spatulae. The combination of these features creates strong yet reversible adhesion through van der Waals forces. Researchers have harnessed this concept and applied it to create surgical glue that can revolutionize various aspects of healthcare.

The gecko-inspired surgical glue offers several key advantages in healthcare design:

Improved Tissue Adhesion: Traditional surgical adhesives and sutures can sometimes damage delicate tissues, leading to complications and prolonged healing times. Gecko-inspired adhesives provide a gentler, non-invasive solution. By mimicking the gecko's adhesive mechanism, these adhesives can adhere to tissues with remarkable strength, without causing harm.

Minimally Invasive Procedures: The surgical glue allows for minimally invasive procedures, reducing the need for large incisions. This leads to less trauma for patients, faster recovery times, and lower risks of infection and scarring. The glue can be applied through small incisions or even endoscopically, making it ideal for various surgeries.

Enhanced Precision: The gecko-inspired adhesive can be precisely controlled, enabling surgeons to place it exactly where needed. This precision is particularly valuable in delicate surgeries, such as those involving nerves or blood vessels, where traditional adhesives or sutures may be less effective.

Biocompatibility: Biomaterials used in these adhesives are often biocompatible and safe for use within the human body. This ensures that the glue does not elicit an immune response or cause allergic reactions, making it suitable for a wide range of medical applications.

Reduced Healing Time: Faster tissue adhesion and less trauma translate into shorter healing times for patients. This is especially beneficial for procedures that involve critical organs or structures, as it can lead to quicker recovery and reduced post-operative complications.

Versatile Applications: The gecko-inspired surgical glue is not limited to a single medical field. It finds applications in various surgical disciplines, such as neurosurgery, cardiac surgery, ophthalmology, and even in wound closure. Its versatility makes it a valuable addition to the healthcare toolkit.

The development of gecko-inspired surgical glue is just one example of how biomaterials and bio systems are transforming healthcare design. As researchers continue to explore nature-inspired solutions, we can expect even more innovative approaches to improve medical procedures, enhance patient comfort, and ultimately, save lives. This marriage of biology and technology offers a promising glimpse into the future of healthcare and medical innovation.

Applications of Biomaterials and Bio systems in Health care design Robotics

Biomaterials and bio systems have revolutionized the field of healthcare design and robotics. These versatile materials and systems have found a wide range of applications, enhancing the performance and capabilities of medical devices and robotic systems. The convergence of these technologies has paved the way for innovative solutions that improve patient care, surgical procedures, and overall healthcare delivery. Here, we explore some of the key applications of biomaterials and bio systems in healthcare design and robotics.

Implantable Medical Devices:

Biomaterials play a pivotal role in the development of implantable medical devices such as artificial joints, dental implants, and cardiac stents. These materials are chosen for their compatibility with biological tissues, durability, and corrosion resistance. They ensure the long-term success of such implants, enabling patients to regain mobility and health. Moreover, bio systems can be integrated into these devices to monitor and transmit real-time data, allowing for remote patient monitoring and improved healthcare outcomes.

Drug Delivery Systems:

Biomaterials are widely employed in drug delivery systems to control the release of medications within the body. By using biocompatible polymers and nanoparticles, drug delivery systems can be designed to release drugs at a specific rate, time, or location. This precision not only enhances the therapeutic effect but also reduces side effects. Bio systems can be incorporated to fine-tune drug release based on real-time physiological data, optimizing treatment outcomes.

Tissue Engineering and Regenerative Medicine:

The development of biomaterials and bio systems has opened up exciting possibilities in tissue engineering and regenerative medicine. Scaffolds made from biocompatible materials provide a framework for the growth of new tissues and organs, addressing the shortage of donor organs. Bio systems can be used to monitor and stimulate tissue growth, ensuring the development of functional and viable replacement tissues. This approach has the potential to revolutionize organ transplantation and repair damaged tissues.

Surgical Robotics:

Robotic systems have gained prominence in the field of healthcare, especially in surgical procedures. Biomaterials are utilized in the construction of robotic components to provide strength, lightness, and resistance to wear and tear. Robotic-assisted surgeries are increasingly becoming more precise, less invasive, and safer for patients. These systems are also capable of integrating biosensors and real-time imaging systems, providing surgeons with enhanced vision and control during procedures.

Assistive Devices for Rehabilitation:

Biomaterials and bio systems have significantly contributed to the development of assistive devices for rehabilitation. Prosthetic limbs, orthotic braces, and exoskeletons employ advanced materials that mimic natural biological movements and enhance patient mobility. Bio systems can be integrated into these devices to provide sensory feedback to users, enhancing their sense of proprioception and control.

Healthcare Monitoring and Diagnosis:

Bio systems, such as wearable sensors and diagnostic devices, have enabled continuous monitoring of patients' vital signs, blood glucose levels, and other health parameters. These systems provide valuable data that can be used for early detection of medical conditions and timely interventions. Furthermore, they can transmit data to healthcare professionals, allowing for remote patient management and personalized care.

The integration of biomaterials and bio systems in healthcare design and robotics has ushered in a new era of innovative solutions that enhance patient care, improve surgical outcomes, and enable a more personalized approach to healthcare. The synergy of these technologies continues to drive advancements in medical devices, surgical robotics, and patient monitoring, ultimately contributing to the betterment of healthcare and the well-being of individuals worldwide.

Applications of Biomaterials and Bio systems in Health care design Marine

Biomaterials and bio systems have revolutionized the field of healthcare design, providing innovative solutions and materials for a wide range of medical applications. While much attention has been focused on terrestrial healthcare, the potential applications of biomaterials and bio systems in marine healthcare settings are equally significant. This article explores the unique challenges and opportunities in integrating biomaterials and bio systems into marine healthcare design.

Medical Devices for Underwater Medicine:

One of the most intriguing applications of biomaterials and bio systems in marine healthcare design involves the development of medical devices for underwater medicine. These devices must withstand the harsh conditions of the marine environment, such as high pressure, salinity, and corrosion. Specialized biomaterials, like biocompatible polymers and corrosion-resistant alloys, are essential for creating medical devices that can be used in underwater healthcare scenarios. These devices can support activities such as underwater surgeries, wound care, and diagnostic procedures for aquatic creatures or human divers.

Marine Tissue Engineering:

The marine environment is home to a diverse range of species, some of which possess unique regenerative capabilities. Biomaterials play a crucial role in marine tissue engineering, enabling scientists to develop materials and scaffolds that mimic the native tissues of marine organisms. These biomaterials can be used for the repair and regeneration of damaged tissues in marine species, including coral reefs and endangered marine animals. By harnessing the power of bio systems, researchers can work towards restoring and preserving marine ecosystems.

Waterborne Drug Delivery Systems:

Biomaterials and bio systems are also instrumental in the development of innovative drug delivery systems designed for marine healthcare applications. These systems can be employed for targeted drug delivery to marine organisms, both for therapeutic and conservation purposes. For example, controlled-release biomaterials can deliver antibiotics to treat infections in aquatic species or release nutrients to support coral reef restoration efforts. Such systems can be tailored to the specific needs of the marine environment, ensuring the safety and efficacy of treatments.

Bio-Inspired Underwater Sensors:

Bio systems are a rich source of inspiration for the design of underwater sensors and monitoring devices. Marine ecosystems are highly sensitive to environmental changes, and bio-inspired sensors can help scientists and conservationists gather data on water quality, temperature, and the presence of pollutants. Biomaterials play a role in the development of sensor coatings and materials that can resist fouling and bio fouling in underwater environments, ensuring accurate and long-term data collection.

Marine Biocompatible Implants:

Just as biomaterials have been used for medical implants in humans, they can be employed for marine species as well. For instance, biocompatible implants can aid in tracking and studying the behaviour of marine animals, including fish and sea mammals. By integrating advanced biomaterials and bio systems into these implants, researchers can gain valuable insights into the migratory patterns and health of these species.

The integration of biomaterials and bio systems into marine healthcare design holds great promise for both therapeutic and ecological applications. The unique challenges of the marine environment require innovative solutions that can withstand extreme conditions while providing effective healthcare solutions for marine organisms and ecosystems. By exploring these applications, we can contribute to the conservation of our oceans and the well-being of the creatures that inhabit them, ultimately advancing the field of marine healthcare design.

<u>Applications of Biomaterials and Bio systems in Health care design Aeronautical.</u>

Biomaterials and bio systems play a pivotal role in revolutionizing both healthcare and aeronautical industries, offering innovative solutions that enhance safety, performance, and sustainability. These materials and systems are designed to interact with biological entities, and their applications span a wide range of medical and aerospace disciplines. Here, we explore the multifaceted applications of biomaterials and bio systems in these two domains.

Healthcare Applications:

Implantable Medical Devices: Biomaterials are used to create medical implants, such as artificial joints, pacemakers, and dental implants. These materials must be biocompatible, corrosion-resistant, and strong to ensure patient safety and longevity.

Tissue Engineering: Biomaterials, including biodegradable polymers and scaffolds, are used to create tissue-engineered constructs. These constructs aid in regenerating damaged tissues and organs, offering hope for patients in need of transplants or tissue repair.

Drug Delivery Systems: Nanotechnology-based biomaterials enable the controlled release of drugs, improving therapeutic efficacy and reducing side effects. These systems are particularly useful in cancer treatment and chronic disease management.

Biocompatible Coatings: Biomaterials can be used to create biocompatible coatings for medical equipment and instruments. These coatings reduce the risk of infection and improve patient outcomes.

Wound Dressings: Biomaterial-based wound dressings with antimicrobial properties promote faster healing and reduce the risk of infection in patients with chronic wounds.

Aeronautical Applications:

Lightweight Composites: The aerospace industry benefits from lightweight biomaterial composites. These materials, inspired by the strength and lightweight characteristics of natural materials, reduce the weight of aircraft and enhance fuel efficiency.

Aero elastic Tailoring: Biomimicry is used to design aircraft structures that mimic the flexibility and adaptability of biological systems. This allows aircraft to adapt to different flight conditions, improving performance and safety.

Biofuel Development: Biomaterials play a role in developing sustainable aviation biofuels. Algae-based biofuels, for example, offer a renewable and eco-friendly alternative to traditional aviation fuels.

Biologically-Inspired Design: Aircraft design often takes inspiration from nature, leading to innovations like wing morphing and quieter flight. Biomimetic design principles enhance aircraft efficiency and reduce environmental impact.

Space Travel and Life Support Systems: In space exploration, biomaterials and bio systems are used in life support systems, food production, and waste recycling. These technologies are crucial for long-duration space missions.

The convergence of healthcare and aeronautical design in the development of bio systems and biomaterials has led to remarkable innovations. These materials and systems not only improve patient outcomes in healthcare but also contribute to safer, more efficient, and environmentally sustainable aviation practices. The on-going research and development in these fields promise even more ground breaking applications that will continue to shape the future of both industries.

CHAPTER THREE

BIO SUSTAINABLE DEVELOPMENT

Innovations in Energy (Termite mound inspired shopping malls), Innovations in Resource-Air (purification, filtration), Dew water collection systems, water purification, desalination, Management of spaces, designs for megastructures.

Innovations in Energy (Termite mound inspired shopping malls)

Innovations in energy are at the forefront of modern technological advancements, as the world grapples with the need for sustainable and efficient energy sources. One fascinating and innovative concept that has emerged is the idea of drawing inspiration from nature, specifically termite mounds, to design energy-efficient structures such as shopping malls.

Termite mounds are remarkable structures built by these tiny insects in arid regions, serving as their homes. What makes termite mounds so intriguing is their ability to regulate temperature and humidity within the mound, creating a stable and comfortable environment for the termites. This natural phenomenon has inspired architects and engineers to explore how these principles can be applied to human-made structures, including shopping malls.

One key innovation is the integration of passive cooling and ventilation systems modelled after termite mounds. Termite mounds have a network of tunnels and chambers that facilitate airflow, allowing for efficient temperature regulation. Similarly, modern buildings, including shopping malls, are being designed with carefully planned ventilation systems that reduce the reliance on energy-intensive air conditioning. These systems harness natural air currents and employ smart architectural features to maintain comfortable temperatures while reducing energy consumption.

Furthermore, termite mounds have optimized shapes and materials that contribute to their thermal efficiency. Architects are experimenting with biomimicry, using similar shapes and materials to design shopping malls that are not only aesthetically pleasing but also energy-efficient. These structures often feature innovative designs that incorporate passive solar heating and cooling elements, as well as reflective surfaces to minimize heat absorption.

Another aspect of termite mounds that has inspired innovation in energy efficiency is their ability to capture and store water. In arid environments, termites collect moisture from the air and store it in chambers within the mound. This concept has led to the development of systems that capture rainwater and humidity for use in cooling and irrigation in shopping mall environments. This reduces the reliance on traditional water sources and supports sustainable practices.

Moreover, some shopping malls are exploring the use of advanced materials that mimic the natural insulation properties of termite mound materials. These materials can help maintain a stable temperature within the building, reducing the need for energy-consuming heating or cooling systems. By using well-insulated materials, shopping malls can decrease their energy consumption and environmental impact.

Innovations in energy efficiency, inspired by the remarkable designs of termite mounds, are transforming the way we construct and operate buildings, including shopping malls. By integrating passive cooling and ventilation systems, optimizing shapes and materials, and harnessing nature's water-capturing abilities, these structures are becoming more sustainable and environmentally friendly. Termite-inspired shopping malls are not only a testament to human creativity but also a step toward a greener and more sustainable future in the world of architecture and energy conservation.

Innovations in Resource-Air (purification, filtration)

Innovations in resource-air purification and filtration have seen significant advancements in recent years, driven by the increasing awareness of air quality concerns and the need to address environmental challenges. These innovations have the potential to improve the quality of the air we breathe and have a positive impact on public health and the environment.

Nanotechnology Applications:

Nanotechnology has played a crucial role in the development of advanced air purification and filtration systems. Nanoparticles, such as titanium dioxide and carbon nanotubes, have been used to create highly efficient filters. These materials can capture and break down pollutants at the molecular level, providing improved air quality and reducing the release of harmful compounds into the atmosphere.

Smart and IoT-Enabled Devices:

Innovations in air purification and filtration include the integration of smart and Internet of Things (IoT) technologies. These devices can monitor air quality in real-time and adjust their operation accordingly. Users can control these systems remotely through their smartphones, ensuring that indoor air remains clean and healthy. These innovations not only enhance convenience but also enable efficient energy usage.

Electrostatic Precipitators:

Electrostatic precipitators are advanced filtration systems that use electric charges to remove particles from the air. They are highly effective in capturing even the smallest particles, including fine dust and pollutants. The development of smaller and more efficient electrostatic precipitators has made them more accessible for residential use.

UV-C and Photo catalytic Oxidation:

Ultraviolet-C (UV-C) light and photo catalytic oxidation have gained popularity for their ability to eliminate airborne pathogens, including viruses and bacteria. UV-C lamps and photo catalytic coatings can be integrated into air purifiers and HVAC systems, providing an extra layer of protection against biological contaminants.

Natural and Green Solutions:

In addition to technological innovations, there is a growing interest in natural and green air purification methods. This includes the use of indoor plants, which can help remove certain pollutants and improve air quality. Additionally, developments in bioremediation technologies harness the power of microorganisms to break down pollutants in the air.

Air Filtration in High-Risk Environments:

Innovations in air filtration have extended beyond residential and commercial settings to high-risk environments such as hospitals and laboratories. High-efficiency particulate air (HEPA) filters, antimicrobial coatings, and specialized ventilation systems have become essential tools for maintaining clean and sterile air in these critical spaces.

Portable and Wearable Devices:

The development of portable and wearable air purification devices has allowed individuals to carry clean air with them wherever they go. These compact devices can be worn as masks or carried in bags, offering personal protection against pollutants, allergens, and pathogens.

Sustainable and Eco-Friendly Filtration:

Eco-friendly filtration materials and sustainable design principles are increasingly being incorporated into air purification systems. Biodegradable filters and systems that consume minimal energy are becoming more popular, aligning with the global focus on reducing the environmental footprint of such technologies.

Innovations in resource-air purification and filtration have evolved to address the ever-growing concerns about air quality and its impact on health and the environment. These advancements encompass various approaches, from nanotechnology and smart devices to natural solutions and sustainable designs. As technology continues to advance, air purification and filtration systems will play a vital role in ensuring cleaner and healthier air for all.

Innovations in Resource-Dew water collection systems

Water scarcity is a pressing global challenge, with millions of people around the world facing limited access to clean and safe drinking water. In response to this crisis, innovative solutions have emerged to harness alternative sources of water, and one such solution is the development of dew water collection systems. Dew, the moisture that forms on surfaces overnight or during periods of low humidity, represents a largely untapped source of freshwater. Innovations in dew water collection systems have the potential to provide a sustainable and reliable source of clean water in regions where conventional sources are limited or contaminated.

Dew Harvesting Materials:

Recent innovations in materials have significantly improved the efficiency of dew water collection systems. Super hydrophobic surfaces, which have a high affinity for water droplets, have been developed to enhance dew condensation. These surfaces allow dew to form more readily and facilitate the collection of larger quantities of water. Researchers have also explored the use of special coatings and materials, such as hydrogels and nanomaterial's, to enhance the dew collection process.

Passive Collection Systems:

Traditional dew water collection systems often require energy-intensive processes, such as refrigeration or active condensation. However, recent innovations focus on passive collection systems that operate without external energy sources. One approach involves using radioactive cooling, where surfaces are designed to emit heat into the cold night sky, promoting dew formation. This passive approach reduces the energy consumption associated with dew harvesting systems, making them more sustainable and cost-effective.

Atmospheric Water Generators (AWGs):

Atmospheric water generators have gained popularity as a dew water collection technology. These systems utilize refrigeration and condensation processes to extract moisture from the air, which can then be used for various purposes. Innovations in AWGs have led to increased efficiency and portability, making them suitable for both urban and rural settings. Additionally, some AWGs incorporate solar panels to power their operation, reducing their environmental impact.

Data-Driven Dew Water Collection:

Advancements in data analytics and meteorological modelling have enabled more accurate predictions of dew formation and collection potential in specific locations. By analysing historical weather patterns, temperature fluctuations, and humidity levels, these systems can optimize the timing and positioning of dew water collection devices. This data-driven approach ensures that dew harvesting systems are deployed effectively, maximizing their water yield.

Integration with Existing Infrastructure:

Innovative dew water collection systems are being designed to integrate seamlessly with existing infrastructure. For example, some buildings incorporate dew harvesting materials into their architectural designs, enabling the passive collection of dew on rooftops and walls. This approach not only makes efficient use of available space but also complements other water sources, such as rainwater harvesting systems.

Environmental Sustainability:

Environmental considerations are increasingly central to the development of dew water collection technologies. Innovations in eco-friendly materials, such as non-toxic coatings and recyclable components, ensure that these systems have a minimal ecological footprint. Additionally, some designs incorporate sustainable energy sources like solar panels and wind turbines to power the dew collection process.

Innovations in resource-dew water collection systems offer a promising solution to address the growing global water scarcity challenge. These systems utilize advanced materials, passive collection techniques, and data-driven approaches to maximize water yield while minimizing environmental impact. By harnessing the moisture that nature provides through dew, we can contribute to a more sustainable and resilient water supply for communities facing water shortages and environmental stress.

Innovations in Resource- water purification

Innovations in water purification have played a crucial role in ensuring access to clean and safe drinking water, addressing water scarcity, and mitigating environmental pollution. These innovations have evolved over the years, driven by the need to provide clean water for growing populations and the increasing awareness of the importance of safeguarding water resources. While I can't provide specific examples post-2022, I can highlight some general trends and innovations in water purification that were relevant at the time of my last knowledge update.

Membrane Filtration Technologies: Membrane filtration techniques such as reverse osmosis and ultrafiltration have been significant innovations in water purification. These methods use semipermeable membranes to separate impurities from water, ensuring the removal of particles, bacteria, and even some dissolved ions and molecules.

Advanced Oxidation Processes: Advanced oxidation processes (AOPs) involve the use of powerful oxidants such as ozone, UV light, or hydrogen peroxide to break down and remove organic and inorganic contaminants in water. AOPs are effective at treating complex pollutants and emerging contaminants.

Nanotechnology: Nanotechnology has introduced the use of nanomaterial's and nanoscale processes to enhance water treatment. Nanomaterial's like carbon nanotubes, graphene, and nanoparticles are employed to remove contaminants and improve the efficiency of water purification systems.

Desalination Technologies: As freshwater sources become scarcer, desalination technologies have gained prominence. Innovations in desalination processes, including reverse osmosis, multi-effect distillation, and forward osmosis, have made seawater and brackish water desalination more energy-efficient and cost-effective.

Solar Water Purification: Solar-powered water purification systems have been developed to provide clean drinking water in remote or off-grid areas. These systems use solar energy to power processes like distillation, UV disinfection, or membrane filtration, making them sustainable and environmentally friendly.

Mobile and Point-of-Use Systems: Portable water purification devices and point-of-use systems have become essential in emergency situations and for providing access to clean water in rural or underserved areas. These systems often rely on innovative filtration and disinfection methods.

Electrochemical Water Treatment: Electrochemical techniques, such as electrocoagulation and electro chlorination, have been developed to remove contaminants and pathogens from water by using electricity. These methods can be more energy-efficient and cost-effective than traditional chemical treatments.

Smart Water Purification Systems: The integration of sensors, data analytics, and automation in water purification processes has improved efficiency and reliability. Smart systems can monitor water quality in real-time and adjust treatment processes accordingly, reducing waste and energy consumption.

Biologically-Based Water Treatment: Innovations in bioremediation and phytoremediation use natural processes and living organisms to remove contaminants from water. These methods can be environmentally sustainable and cost-effective for certain types of water treatment.

3D-Printed Water Filters: 3D printing technology has enabled the design and production of customized water filtration systems. These systems can be tailored to specific water quality and supply challenges.

Innovations in water purification have been instrumental in addressing water quality and scarcity issues around the world. These advancements continue to evolve, offering new possibilities for providing clean and safe drinking water to communities while minimizing the environmental impact of water treatment processes. It's important to note that on-going research and development in this field may have introduced even more exciting innovations beyond my last knowledge update in early 2022.

Innovations in Resource- desalination

Innovations in resource desalination have emerged as a critical solution to address the world's growing water scarcity issues. Desalination is the process of removing salt and other impurities from seawater or brackish water to make it suitable for human consumption, agriculture, and industrial use. As fresh water sources become increasingly stressed due to population growth, climate change, and over-exploitation, the development of innovative desalination technologies has become essential in ensuring a sustainable and reliable source of freshwater.

One significant innovation in desalination is the advancement of membrane-based technologies. Reverse osmosis (RO) and Nano filtration membranes have become more efficient and cost-effective over the years. These membranes are capable of filtering out salts and impurities, leaving behind clean and potable water. The development of high-performance membranes with enhanced fouling resistance and durability has significantly improved the energy efficiency of the desalination process, reducing the overall environmental impact.

Furthermore, the integration of renewable energy sources into desalination processes is another promising innovation. Traditional desalination methods, such as multi-effect distillation and thermal processes, often consume vast amounts of energy, primarily derived from fossil fuels. However, the utilization of solar, wind, and other renewable energy sources to power desalination plants has gained traction. Solar desalination, in particular, is becoming increasingly popular in regions with abundant sunlight. This approach not only reduces the carbon footprint of desalination but also makes the process more sustainable and economically viable in the long run.

Innovations in desalination also include improvements in water recovery rates. Zero-liquid discharge (ZLD) technologies have gained attention as they aim to minimize water wastage by recovering nearly all the water from the desalination process. ZLD systems are particularly relevant in areas where freshwater resources are scarce, as they can help reduce the environmental impact and alleviate water stress.

Additionally, innovations in desalination have led to the exploration of alternative water sources. For example, brine management and resource recovery technologies are being developed to extract valuable minerals and chemicals from the brine generated during desalination, turning a waste product into a resource. These technologies have the potential to make desalination not only a source of freshwater but also a sustainable source of raw materials.

Desalination innovations are not limited to technological advancements alone. Improved water governance, policy frameworks, and international collaborations have played a crucial role in making desalination projects more feasible and sustainable. Countries and regions are now working together to develop shared desalination facilities and distribution networks, optimizing resource allocation and reducing the overall environmental impact.

Innovations in resource desalination have transformed this technology from a costly and energy-intensive process into a more sustainable and viable solution for addressing water scarcity. Advancements in membrane technologies, integration of renewable energy, improved water recovery rates, and responsible brine management are all contributing to a more efficient, environmentally friendly, and economically feasible approach to desalination. As water scarcity continues to be a global challenge, the on-going development of innovative desalination solutions is of paramount importance in securing our access to freshwater resources.

<u>**Innovations in Resource- Management of spaces**</u>

Innovations in resource management of spaces have become increasingly important in a world characterized by rapid urbanization, environmental challenges, and the need for more efficient and sustainable use of resources. These innovations encompass a wide range of strategies and technologies that aim to optimize the utilization of physical spaces while minimizing the negative impact on the environment. Here, we'll explore some key trends and developments in resource management of spaces.

Smart Building Technology: Smart buildings are equipped with various sensors and automation systems that collect and analyse data to optimize energy use, security, and space utilization. These technologies can adjust lighting, heating, and cooling based on occupancy, monitor air quality, and even predict maintenance needs, leading to significant resource savings.

Flexible Workspace Design: The rise of flexible working arrangements has led to the development of adaptable office spaces. These environments can be reconfigured to meet changing needs, reducing the overall space required and, in turn, lowering overhead costs. This approach also promotes collaboration and innovation among employees.

IoT and Sensors: The Internet of Things (IoT) is playing a vital role in resource management. Sensors embedded in various spaces can monitor usage patterns, detect inefficiencies, and trigger automated responses. For instance, smart lighting systems can adjust brightness and turn off lights in unoccupied areas, conserving energy.

Space Sharing Platforms: The sharing economy has extended to the realm of real estate. Platforms like Airbnb and We Work enable individuals and businesses to share their unused spaces, generating income and making more efficient use of underutilized resources.

Green Building Practices: Sustainable building practices have become a standard in construction. Innovations in energy-efficient design, renewable energy integration, and green materials reduce the environmental footprint of buildings. Green roofs, for instance, improve insulation and absorb rainwater, contributing to better resource management.

Space Optimization Software: Advanced software tools are now available to help organizations analyse space utilization. By studying data on how spaces are used, companies can make informed decisions about downsizing, reconfiguring, or optimizing their facilities to reduce costs and environmental impact.

Waste Reduction Strategies: Efficient resource management extends to waste reduction. Recycling and composting programs in shared spaces, such as apartment complexes or offices, help minimize the environmental impact of waste disposal.

Urban Planning and Smart Cities: At the city level, urban planners are integrating resource management into their designs. Smart cities use data and technology to optimize traffic flow, reduce energy consumption, and enhance the quality of life for residents.

Energy and Water Management: Innovations in energy and water management help reduce resource consumption in spaces. Building automation systems can regulate heating, cooling, and lighting, while advanced water monitoring systems can detect leaks and promote water conservation.

Collaborative Resource Management: Collaborative platforms enable communities and organizations to collectively manage and share resources, from vehicles to meeting spaces, reducing the need for individual ownership and, in turn, the environmental impact.

Innovations in resource management of spaces are not only about cost reduction but also about sustainability and environmental stewardship. By harnessing technology, data, and forward-thinking design, individuals, businesses, and cities can create more efficient and eco-friendly spaces that meet the demands of a rapidly changing world. These innovations are not only addressing resource scarcity but also promoting a better quality of life for all.

<u>Innovations in Resource- designs for mega structures.</u>

Innovations in resource-efficient designs for megastructures have become a crucial area of focus in modern architecture and engineering. Megastructures, often defined as exceptionally large and complex buildings or infrastructural projects, pose unique challenges and opportunities for sustainability and resource optimization. These innovations are driven by the need to address the growing global population and urbanization, while also mitigating the environmental impact of such colossal constructions.

Sustainable Materials:

One of the primary areas of innovation in megastructures design is the utilization of sustainable building materials. Traditional construction materials like concrete and steel are resource-intensive and contribute significantly to greenhouse gas emissions. Innovators are exploring alternative materials, such as bamboo, engineered wood, and even recycled plastics, to reduce the environmental footprint of megastructures. These materials are not only eco-friendly but also lightweight, durable, and cost-effective.

Modular and Prefabricated Construction:

Modular and prefabricated construction techniques are gaining traction in megastructures design. This approach involves constructing building components off-site and assembling them on location. It minimizes waste, reduces construction time, and enhances resource efficiency. Moreover, it allows for flexibility in design and easy disassembly, enabling the repurposing of materials for future projects.

Energy Efficiency and Green Technologies:

Incorporating energy-efficient systems and green technologies is another key innovation in megastructures design. These include advanced insulation, efficient HVAC systems, renewable energy sources (solar panels, wind turbines), and smart building management systems. These innovations can significantly reduce energy consumption, carbon emissions, and long-term operational costs.

Vertical Farming and Green Spaces:

Megastructures in urban environments are embracing vertical farming and green spaces to enhance sustainability. These innovations promote food production within the structure itself, reducing the need for transportation and the environmental impact of conventional agriculture. Green spaces not only improve air quality but also provide recreational areas for occupants, contributing to their overall well-being.

Water Management:

Efficient water management is crucial in megastructures. Innovations in water recycling and rainwater harvesting systems reduce the demand on external water sources. Additionally, the treatment and reuse of wastewater can contribute to resource conservation and sustainable water practices.

Adaptive Design:

Adaptive designs are becoming more common in megastructures, allowing for flexible usage and occupancy. These structures can evolve and adapt to changing needs, reducing the need for complete overhauls or demolitions. Such designs maximize the lifespan of the megastructures and reduce waste.

3D Printing and Robotics:

Advanced technologies like 3D printing and robotics are transforming the construction industry. These technologies enable precise, on-demand construction, reducing material waste and labour requirements. In megastructures design, they offer the potential for creating complex and sustainable structures with a high degree of precision.

Data-driven Design and Simulation:

Data-driven design and simulation tools are being used to optimize the resource efficiency of megastructures. These technologies allow architects and engineers to analyse various scenarios and make informed decisions regarding energy consumption, material usage, and overall sustainability.

Innovations in resource-efficient designs for megastructures are essential to address the growing challenges of urbanization and environmental sustainability. By incorporating sustainable materials, modular construction, energy-efficient systems, green technologies, and more, megastructures can not only be impressive architectural feats but also environmentally responsible and adaptable solutions for the future. These innovations are shaping the way we approach the design and construction of large-scale buildings and infrastructure, promoting a more sustainable and resilient built environment.

CHAPTER FOUR

BIO COMPUTING AND OPTIMISATION

No Free Lunch Theorem, Bat Algorithm, Flower Pollination Algorithm, Genetic Algorithm- Crossover and Mutation Operations. Bio-Inspired Optimisation, Ant Colony Optimisation (ACO), Swam Intelligence- Particle Swam Optimisation (PSO).

No Free Lunch Theorem

Bioinformatics, which combines biology and computer science, has emerged as a powerful field for analysing biological data and optimizing various biological processes. Within this domain, the "No Free Lunch Theorem" holds a significant place, as it provides a fundamental understanding of the limitations and challenges faced in bioinformatics and optimization.

The "No Free Lunch Theorem" (NFL) is a concept originally introduced in the field of machine learning and optimization. It can be applied to a wide range of fields, including bioinformatics. Essentially, the theorem suggests that no single optimization or search algorithm is universally superior to all others across all possible problems. In other words, there is no one-size-fits-all algorithm that can guarantee the best performance for every possible biological problem or data set.

This theorem underscores the importance of algorithm selection and adaptation in the context of bioinformatics and optimization. Since there is no universally optimal approach, researchers in bioinformatics must carefully choose or design algorithms that are specifically suited to the characteristics of their biological data and the nature of the problem they are trying to solve. This highlights the need for domain-specific knowledge and expertise in bioinformatics.

For example, when dealing with DNA sequence alignment, one algorithm may perform exceptionally well, while it may not be as effective in protein structure prediction. Conversely, an algorithm designed for optimizing metabolic pathways may not be suitable for predicting gene expression patterns. Each problem in bioinformatics is unique, and choosing the right algorithm is crucial for achieving accurate and meaningful results.

The "No Free Lunch Theorem" also serves as a reminder of the on-going need for innovation and adaptation in the field of bioinformatics. Researchers should continually explore new algorithms and techniques to address the evolving challenges posed by biological data. Furthermore, they should be open to modifying and tailoring existing algorithms to better suit specific biological problems, as no single method can claim to be universally superior.

The "No Free Lunch Theorem" is a fundamental concept in bioinformatics and optimization, emphasizing the importance of algorithm selection and adaptation. While it acknowledges the absence of a one-size-fits-all solution, it motivates researchers to continually refine and innovate in their pursuit of more effective and accurate methods for solving complex biological problems.

Bat Algorithm

Bio-computing and optimization are fascinating fields that draw inspiration from nature to solve complex problems. One such algorithm in this realm is the Bat Algorithm, which takes its cues from the echolocation behaviour of bats. Developed by Xin-She Yang in 2010, the Bat Algorithm is a heuristic search and optimization algorithm designed for finding optimal solutions in various problem domains.

Principle of the Bat Algorithm:

The Bat Algorithm is based on the biological behaviour of bats, particularly their ability to emit high-frequency sounds (ultrasonic pulses) and use the echoes to locate prey or obstacles. This process, known as echolocation, serves as the fundamental concept behind the algorithm.

In the context of optimization, the Bat Algorithm works by mimicking the following principles:

Emission of Frequency Pulses: Bats emit ultrasonic pulses at random frequencies when searching for prey. In the algorithm, these pulses represent potential solutions to the optimization problem. Each bat generates a solution, and the quality of the solution corresponds to the loudness of the emitted pulse.

Local Search and Exploration: Bats exhibit two fundamental behaviours when echo locating: local search and exploration. Local search refers to the bats' ability to adjust their emitted frequencies to hone in on a potential target. In the Bat Algorithm, this corresponds to improving a solution in the vicinity of the current best solution. Exploration, on the other hand, involves bats emitting pulses at random frequencies to explore new areas. This aids in escaping local optima.

Frequency and Loudness: The frequency and loudness of the emitted pulses are important parameters in the algorithm. Bats can adjust the frequency and loudness of their calls based on their experience. In the algorithm, the frequency represents how far the bat explores, and the loudness reflects the quality of the solution. These parameters change over time as the algorithm iteratively refines its search.

Algorithm Workflow:

Initialize a population of bats with random solutions to the optimization problem.

Evaluate the fitness of each bat's solution based on the objective function.

Update the frequency and loudness of each bat's emission based on their current solutions and best solutions found so far.

Emit ultrasonic pulses (solutions) based on the updated frequency and loudness.

Evaluate the fitness of the newly generated solutions.

Compare the fitness of the new solutions with the current best solution. If a new solution is better, replace the current best solution with it.

Repeat the above steps for a predefined number of iterations or until convergence criteria are met.

Advantages and Applications:

The Bat Algorithm has gained popularity due to its ability to effectively handle optimization problems with various complexities. Some of its advantages and applications include:

Global Search: The algorithm is well-suited for global optimization problems, as it balances between local exploitation and global exploration.

Flexibility: It can be adapted for various problem domains by customizing the parameters and fitness functions.

Multimodal Optimization: The Bat Algorithm can efficiently locate multiple optimal solutions, making it suitable for multimodal optimization problems.

Real-world Applications: It has been applied to diverse fields, including engineering design, image processing, financial modelling, and data clustering.

The Bat Algorithm is a bio-inspired optimization technique that leverages the echolocation behaviour of bats to efficiently solve complex optimization problems. Its ability to strike a balance between exploration and exploitation makes it a valuable tool in the field of bio-computing and optimization.

Flower Pollination Algorithm

Bio-computing and optimization algorithms draw inspiration from various natural processes and organisms to solve complex computational problems efficiently. One such algorithm is the Flower Pollination Algorithm (FPA). FPA is a nature-inspired optimization technique that mimics the process of pollination in flowering plants. This algorithm was introduced by Xin-She Yang in 2012 and has gained popularity for its simplicity and effectiveness in solving optimization problems.

The Flower Pollination Algorithm is based on the idea of modelling the foraging behaviour of flowers and their pollinators, such as bees and butterflies. The algorithm is designed to search for optimal solutions by simulating the pollination process and the movement of pollinators among flowers. It can be applied to a wide range of optimization problems, including function optimization, engineering design, and other domains where finding the best solution is essential.

The main components and steps of the Flower Pollination Algorithm can be summarized as follows:

Initialization: In the first step, a population of potential solutions, or "flowers," is randomly generated. Each flower represents a candidate solution to the optimization problem.

Evaluation: The fitness of each flower is determined by evaluating its objective function. The objective function measures how well a particular solution performs with respect to the problem's constraints and goals.

Pollination: The algorithm simulates the pollination process by allowing flowers to share information with one another. Flowers with higher fitness values are considered better solutions and are more likely to attract pollinators.

Local search: Some flowers engage in local search to explore their neighbourhoods and potentially improve their fitness. This helps in increasing the diversity of the solutions.

Global search: The algorithm encourages exploration by allowing a few flowers to explore the entire search space, promoting diversity and preventing premature convergence.

Update: The algorithm replaces the less fit flowers with the offspring of the more fit ones, thereby iteratively improving the quality of solutions over multiple generations.

The Flower Pollination Algorithm's key strength lies in its ability to balance exploration and exploitation. By imitating the pollination process, it effectively searches for optimal solutions in a way that combines both global and local search strategies. This makes FPA well-suited for solving complex optimization problems with various characteristics.

The Flower Pollination Algorithm is a bio-inspired optimization technique that emulates the pollination process in flowering plants. It has proven to be a robust and versatile method for solving a wide range of optimization problems and is appreciated for its simplicity and efficiency. Researchers and practitioners have applied the FPA to fields like engineering, finance, and data analysis, where finding optimal solutions is crucial for real-world applications.

Genetic Algorithm- Crossover and Mutation Operations

Biocomputing and optimization are interdisciplinary fields that combine principles from biology and computer science to solve complex problems. One of the key techniques employed in these domains is the Genetic Algorithm (GA). GAs is a class of optimization algorithms inspired by the process of natural selection and genetics. They have proven to be effective in solving a wide range of optimization problems, and two crucial components of GAs are crossover and mutation operations.

Crossover Operation:

The crossover operation in a genetic algorithm simulates the genetic recombination or mating process in biological evolution. It involves taking two parent solutions and generating one or more offspring by combining their genetic information. There are several methods for performing crossover, including one-point crossover, two-point crossover, uniform crossover, and more.

One-Point Crossover: In this method, a single random point in the parent chromosomes is selected, and the genetic material is exchanged between the parents at that point. This creates two offspring, each inheriting part of their genetic makeup from each parent.

Two-Point Crossover: Similar to one-point crossover, but two points are chosen for genetic material exchange, creating a more diverse set of offspring.

Uniform Crossover: This method randomly selects genes from each parent to form the offspring, providing a higher level of diversity.

Crossover operations allow the algorithm to exploit the best characteristics of both parent solutions and potentially produce improved offspring. It encourages exploration and convergence towards optimal solutions in the search space.

Mutation Operation:

The mutation operation introduces small, random changes into an individual's genetic information, mimicking the mutation process in biological genetics. Mutation helps maintain genetic diversity within the population and prevents premature convergence to suboptimal solutions. While crossover primarily explores and exploits existing genetic material, mutation introduces novelty.

Bit-Flip Mutation: In binary encoding, this method flips individual bits within a chromosome with a certain probability.

Gaussian Mutation: In real-valued encoding, a small random value from a Gaussian distribution is added to a gene with a certain probability.

Swap Mutation: This is often used in permutation problems where two elements in a chromosome are swapped.

Mutation rates are typically low to ensure that the genetic material's integrity is mostly preserved while allowing for occasional random changes. Setting an appropriate mutation rate is crucial, as a high mutation rate can lead to excessive randomness, making it challenging to find optimal solutions.

Both crossover and mutation operations play essential roles in the exploration-exploitation trade-off in genetic algorithms. Crossover allows the algorithm to explore the search space efficiently, while mutation maintains diversity and prevents premature convergence. Properly tuning the parameters associated with these operations is a critical aspect of using genetic algorithms effectively for Biocomputing and optimization tasks, as they can significantly impact the algorithm's performance and convergence to optimal solutions.

Bio-Inspired Optimisation, Ant Colony Optimisation

Bio-Inspired Optimization, specifically Ant Colony Optimization (ACO), is a nature-inspired computational technique that draws its inspiration from the behaviour of ants to solve complex optimization problems. ACO is a part of a broader field known as Swarm Intelligence, which focuses on mimicking the collective and decentralized decision-making processes observed in various natural systems.

Ant Colony Optimization is particularly influenced by the foraging behaviour of real ants. Ants are social insects that exhibit remarkable efficiency in finding the shortest path to food sources. They achieve this by leaving and following chemical pheromone trails. These pheromone trails serve as a means of communication among ants, guiding them towards promising food sources while fading over time.

In the context of optimization problems, ACO mimics this natural behaviour by using a population of artificial ants to explore a solution space. Each ant represents a potential solution, and they construct solutions by iteratively selecting components based on pheromone information and a heuristic function that guides their decision-making. The pheromone levels on various components of solutions are updated as ants traverse the solution space, reflecting the quality of the solutions discovered.

Over time, as ants iteratively explore and refine their paths, better solutions emerge. The pheromone trail is also updated to reinforce paths leading to better solutions and diminish the influence of less promising ones. This dynamic interaction between the exploration of the solution space and the adaptation of pheromone levels leads to the discovery of optimal or near-optimal solutions to complex problems.

Ant Colony Optimization has been successfully applied to a wide range of combinatorial optimization problems, including the Traveling Salesman Problem, Vehicle Routing Problem, and job scheduling. Its effectiveness lies in its ability to find high-quality solutions through a cooperative and decentralized approach, which makes it particularly suitable for problems with a large solution space and complex constraints.

In addition to its problem-solving capabilities, Ant Colony Optimization has been extended and adapted in various ways. For example, different variants of ACO have been developed, including Max-Min Ant System, Ant Colony System, and Elitist Ant System, each with its own modifications to improve performance on specific problem types.

Bio-Inspired Optimization techniques like ACO exemplify the power of emulating natural systems to solve complex problems. By harnessing the principles of self-organization, cooperation, and adaptation observed in ants, ACO has proven to be a valuable tool in addressing optimization challenges across various domains, including logistics, telecommunications, and manufacturing, among others. Its on-going development and application continue to expand the boundaries of what can be achieved through bio-inspired computational methods.

Swam Intelligence- Particle Swam Optimisation

Bio-inspired optimization is a fascinating field of study that draws inspiration from the principles and behaviours observed in biological systems to develop innovative optimization algorithms. Among these bio-inspired methods, Particle Swarm Optimization (PSO) stands out as a powerful and widely used technique. PSO is based on the principles of swarm intelligence, which in turn mimic the collective behaviour of organisms like birds or fish in nature. This approach has proven to be highly effective in solving various optimization problems across different domains.

Swarm intelligence, the underlying concept of PSO, is a collective problem-solving approach based on the behaviour of social organisms and their interactions within a group. It leverages the idea that a group of individuals can achieve better results through cooperation and information sharing. In the context of PSO, the "individuals" are represented by particles in a high-dimensional search space, and their collective movement aims to find the optimal solution to a given problem.

The key principles of Particle Swarm Optimization include:

Position and Velocity: In PSO, each particle has a position and velocity in the search space. These parameters determine the particle's movement within the space and its ability to explore potential solutions.

Social and Cognitive Components: Each particle is influenced by its own experience (cognitive component) and the experiences of its neighbours (social component). This information sharing helps particles adjust their positions and velocities, ultimately converging toward the optimal solution.

Global and Local Bests: Particles keep track of their personal best-known position and the global best-known position among the entire swarm. This allows them to adapt and explore the search space efficiently.

The PSO algorithm iteratively updates the positions and velocities of particles by considering the best solutions found so far. Through this continuous refinement process, the swarm gradually converges toward an optimal or near-optimal solution.

The versatility of PSO is one of its key strengths. It has been successfully applied to a wide range of problems, such as function optimization, parameter tuning in machine learning, network routing, and even financial portfolio optimization. Its efficiency in navigating complex, high-dimensional search spaces makes it an attractive choice for real-world applications.

Particle Swarm Optimization, inspired by the collective behaviour of social organisms, is a powerful bio-inspired optimization algorithm. By mimicking the dynamics of a swarm of particles in search of an optimal solution, PSO has proven to be a valuable tool for addressing a variety of complex optimization problems. Its success lies in its ability to strike a balance between exploration and exploitation of the search space, making it a valuable addition to the toolbox of optimization techniques in a variety of domains.

CHAPTER FIVE

APPLICATIONS OF BIO-INSPIRED INNOVATIONS

Bioinspired innovations in– Automotive, Automation, Materials and Manufacturing, Sensors, Controllers, Communications, Healthcare, Agriculture, food production, and Sports, Environment infrastructure. Carbon Neutral Solutions (Coral Reefs, Eco-cements), Carbon Free Solutions (Lotus leaf inspired paints), Eco restorations (Eco-friendly pesticide).

Bioinspired innovations in– Automotive

Bioinspired innovations in the automotive industry have led to significant advancements in vehicle design, efficiency, and sustainability. Drawing inspiration from nature's ingenious solutions, engineers and designers have developed creative solutions that improve safety, aerodynamics, and fuel efficiency. These innovations not only enhance the performance of automobiles but also contribute to reducing their environmental impact.

Biomimetic Materials: The development of lightweight and high-strength materials inspired by natural substances has revolutionized vehicle manufacturing. For instance, biomimicry has led to the creation of composite materials that mimic the structural integrity of seashells or bones, resulting in vehicles that are both lighter and stronger. This reduces fuel consumption, enhances safety, and lessens the environmental footprint of manufacturing.

Aerodynamics Inspired by Nature: Nature provides a wealth of aerodynamic solutions that have been harnessed to improve vehicle design. For instance, the study of birds and fish has influenced the creation of streamlined vehicle shapes that reduce drag, leading to enhanced fuel efficiency. Biomimetic design also involves developing active aerodynamic features that adjust based on the driving conditions, similar to how birds adjust their wing positions in flight.

Autonomous Vehicles and Swarm Intelligence: The concept of swarm intelligence, inspired by the collective behaviour of social insects like ants, has been applied to the development of autonomous vehicles. These vehicles can communicate with each other and work together efficiently, improving traffic flow and reducing congestion. Moreover, the way ants navigate their environment has inspired algorithms for self-driving cars, improving their ability to sense and adapt to changing road conditions.

Biomimetic Sensors: Nature has inspired the development of sensors that mimic the capabilities of animals, such as bats and insects. These sensors can enhance a vehicle's perception and navigation systems, helping autonomous vehicles operate safely in various environments. For example, echolocation-inspired sensors can assist in obstacle detection and avoidance.

Energy-Efficient Mobility: Learning from the efficient movement of animals like cheetahs and kangaroos, engineers have developed energy-efficient mobility solutions. This includes regenerative braking systems that capture and store energy during braking and then reuse it for acceleration. Additionally, lightweight suspension systems inspired by kangaroo legs can provide a smoother and more energy-efficient ride.

Eco-friendly Coatings and Paints: Bio inspired innovations extend to the development of environmentally friendly coatings and paints for vehicles. Lotus leaves, for example, have inspired the creation of super hydrophobic coatings that repel water and reduce the need for frequent car washes. Similarly, butterfly wings have inspired colour-shifting paints that change their hue based on viewing angles, enhancing aesthetics without the use of harmful chemicals.

Eco-routing Algorithms: Ants and other animals have inspired eco-routing algorithms that help drivers find the most fuel-efficient routes. These algorithms take into account real-time traffic data, road conditions, and other factors, helping drivers reduce fuel consumption and lower their carbon footprint.

Noise Reduction Inspired by Owls: Owls possess extraordinary noise-reduction adaptations in their wings, which have inspired the development of quieter tires and improved aerodynamics. This results in reduced noise pollution and a more comfortable driving experience.

Bio inspired innovations in the automotive industry continue to push the boundaries of design, efficiency, and sustainability. By drawing inspiration from nature's solutions, engineers and designers are not only creating more efficient and safer vehicles but also contributing to a greener and more environmentally responsible future for the automotive sector. These innovations are a testament to the incredible potential of biomimicry in solving complex challenges in the modern world.

<u>**Automation**</u>

Bioinspired innovations in automation represent a fascinating intersection of biology and engineering, where the natural world's principles and mechanisms inspire the development of advanced automated systems. These innovations leverage the evolution-honed solutions that living organisms have developed over millions of years to address various challenges. By emulating nature's strategies, engineers and researchers are creating more efficient, adaptable and sustainable automation technologies across a range of applications.

One remarkable area of bioinspired automation is robotics. Nature has provided a wealth of inspiration for the development of autonomous robots. For instance, the locomotion of animals like birds, insects, and snakes has been mimicked to create robots capable of navigating challenging terrains with remarkable agility. These bioinspired robotic systems not only replicate the biomechanical principles of their biological counterparts but also adapt and learn from their environment, making them invaluable for search and rescue missions, surveillance, and exploration of remote and hazardous environments.

Another example lies in swarm robotics, which draws inspiration from the collective behaviours of social insects such as ants and bees. These autonomous systems operate in large groups and exhibit self-organization, robustness, and scalability, making them ideal for applications like agriculture, disaster response, and environmental monitoring. By emulating the decentralized decision-making of social insects, swarm robotics can achieve complex tasks collaboratively and efficiently.

The field of automation also benefits from bioinspired innovations in the realm of artificial intelligence and machine learning. Neural networks, inspired by the human brain's interconnected neurons, have revolutionized pattern recognition and decision-making in various automation systems. The architecture of convolutional neural networks (CNNs) mimics the visual processing of the human visual cortex, enabling breakthroughs in image and video analysis, including facial recognition and object detection.

Moreover, bioinspired algorithms, such as genetic algorithms and particle swarm optimization, draw inspiration from the process of natural selection and social behaviours observed in birds and fish, respectively. These algorithms are used to optimize complex automation tasks, ranging from logistical planning to resource allocation.

In the context of industrial automation and manufacturing, the study of biomimetics has led to innovations in materials and processes. For instance, researchers have explored the remarkable properties of gecko feet to design adhesives capable of gripping various surfaces without leaving residue. This bioinspired adhesive technology has applications in material handling and assembly automation, where the ability to securely grasp and release objects is critical.

Bio inspired innovations also extend to the optimization of energy-efficient systems. For instance, termite mound-inspired architecture has led to more sustainable building designs that promote natural ventilation and temperature control, reducing the energy consumption of automated climate control systems.

Bioinspired innovations in automation have opened up new frontiers in robotics, artificial intelligence, materials science, and more. By drawing from the incredible diversity of life on Earth, researchers and engineers are continually developing automation technologies that are not only more efficient and adaptable but also environmentally sustainable. This interdisciplinary approach, inspired by the natural world, promises to shape the future of automation in a wide range of applications, improving our quality of life and reducing our environmental footprint.

Bioinspired innovations in–Materials and Manufacturing

Bioinspired innovations in materials and manufacturing have gained significant attention in recent years as researchers and engineers seek new ways to address complex challenges and improve existing processes. Drawing inspiration from nature, these innovations often lead to the development of novel materials, manufacturing techniques, and products that exhibit remarkable properties and performance.

One of the key areas of bioinspired innovation is biomimicry, where designers and engineers look to the natural world for solutions to problems. For example, the lotus leaf's self-cleaning properties have inspired the creation of super hydrophobic materials, which can be used in manufacturing to develop surfaces that repel water and other liquids. This has applications in self-cleaning coatings for various surfaces, such as windows and solar panels, reducing the need for maintenance and cleaning.

Another noteworthy example is the development of lightweight and strong materials inspired by the structure of bones and shells. These materials mimic the hierarchical arrangement of minerals and proteins found in natural composites, resulting in enhanced strength and durability. In manufacturing, this can lead to the production of lighter and more robust components for industries like aerospace and automotive.

In the field of 3D printing, bioinspired designs have contributed to the development of efficient and adaptable structures. For instance, researchers have drawn inspiration from the lattice-like structures of bones to create 3D-printed materials that are both lightweight and strong. Such structures are advantageous in applications where weight reduction is critical, such as in the aerospace industry.

Manufacturing processes have also been improved through bioinspired innovations. The study of spider silk has led to the development of stronger and more flexible synthetic fibres. These fibres can be used in various applications, from textiles to medical devices, as they combine strength and flexibility in a way that few synthetic materials can replicate.

Bioinspired manufacturing techniques are not limited to materials alone. Nature has also influenced the way products are made. For instance, the study of termite mound architecture has led to more efficient and sustainable building designs. The intricate ventilation systems and temperature regulation mechanisms found in termite mounds have inspired new approaches to energy-efficient building design and HVAC systems.

Bioinspired innovations in materials and manufacturing are reshaping industries by harnessing nature's designs and processes. These innovations have led to the creation of advanced materials, manufacturing techniques, and products that are more sustainable, efficient, and capable of addressing complex challenges. As research in this field continues to evolve, we can expect even more ground breaking discoveries that will revolutionize the way we create and utilize materials and manufacturing processes.

Bioinspired innovations in–Sensors

Bioinspired innovations in sensors have revolutionized the field of technology, leading to the development of highly efficient and versatile sensing devices. Drawing inspiration from nature, researchers have been able to create sensors that exhibit remarkable sensitivity, adaptability, and functionality, much like their biological counterparts.

One of the key areas where bioinspired sensors have made significant strides is in mimicking the capabilities of the human olfactory system. The human nose is an incredibly sensitive and selective sensor that can detect a wide range of odours and chemical compounds. By emulating the structure and principles of the olfactory system, engineers have designed electronic noses or "e-noses." These devices utilize arrays of chemical sensors, pattern recognition algorithms, and artificial intelligence to detect and identify various odours and chemical substances. Such bioinspired sensors find applications in environmental monitoring, food quality control, and even medical diagnostics.

Another area of bioinspired sensor innovation focuses on mimicking the visual system of animals and insects. Researchers have developed advanced imaging sensors inspired by the compound eyes of insects like flies and bees. These sensors utilize multiple tiny lenses and photo detectors to capture a wide field of view with excellent motion detection capabilities. These bioinspired sensors are being used in surveillance, autonomous vehicles, and drones for enhanced situational awareness and navigation.

In the field of touch and tactile sensing, bio inspiration from human skin and the mechanoreceptors found in animals has led to the development of highly sensitive and flexible sensors. These sensors can detect various tactile information, including pressure, temperature, and texture. Applications of such bioinspired sensors range from robotics and prosthetics to human-machine interfaces.

Furthermore, the biomimicry of the echolocation abilities of bats has resulted in the creation of bioinspired ultrasonic sensors. These sensors emit ultrasonic waves and analyse the reflected signals to detect objects and measure distances. This technology is employed in various domains, including automotive collision avoidance systems and industrial automation.

In the realm of environmental monitoring, bioinspired sensors have been inspired by various species, such as birds for aerial surveillance and fish for underwater exploration. These sensors can adapt to challenging and dynamic environments, providing valuable data for scientific research, disaster management, and conservation efforts.

Bioinspired sensors have also made significant progress in the healthcare industry. Sensors inspired by the human body, such as glucose monitors and wearable health trackers, have greatly improved the monitoring and management of various medical conditions. These devices can continuously measure physiological parameters and transmit data to healthcare professionals, enabling real-time health assessment and early intervention.

bioinspired innovations in sensors have paved the way for the development of highly advanced and versatile sensing technologies. By drawing inspiration from nature's designs and capabilities, scientists and engineers have created sensors with enhanced sensitivity, adaptability, and functionality, leading to numerous applications across various fields, from environmental monitoring to healthcare and beyond. These bioinspired sensors continue to push the boundaries of what is possible, offering new insights and solutions to complex challenges in the modern world.

Bioinspired innovations in– Controllers

Bioinspired innovations in controllers refer to the development of control systems and algorithms that draw inspiration from nature and living organisms. These bioinspired controllers aim to solve complex problems and improve the efficiency of various applications by emulating biological principles and mechanisms. They can be found in a wide range of fields, from robotics and autonomous systems to industrial automation and healthcare. The key idea behind bioinspired controllers is to harness the power of evolution, adaptation, and biological processes to create intelligent and adaptive control systems.

One prominent example of bioinspired controllers is the use of neural networks and artificial intelligence (AI) techniques that mimic the structure and functioning of the human brain. These controllers can adapt and learn from their environment, making them well-suited for tasks that require flexibility and adaptation. In robotics, for instance, neural network-based controllers have been used to develop robots that can navigate unknown terrain, perform tasks in unstructured environments, and even interact with humans in a more natural and intuitive way.

Another area where bioinspired controllers have made significant advancements is swarm robotics, which takes inspiration from the collective behaviour of social insects like ants and bees. In swarm robotics, a group of simple robots can work together to solve complex tasks, just like a colony of ants collaborates to find food or build structures. Bioinspired algorithms in swarm robotics enable robots to communicate and coordinate their actions, leading to applications in search and rescue missions, environmental monitoring, and even distributed manufacturing.

Bioinspired controllers have also been used in the development of autonomous vehicles and drones. These systems often incorporate principles from animal navigation, such as how birds use magnetic fields for migration or how insects use visual cues for navigation. By emulating these natural mechanisms, autonomous vehicles can enhance their sensing, perception, and decision-making capabilities, ultimately improving their safety and efficiency.

Furthermore, bioinspired controllers are not limited to mimicking animal behaviour. They can also draw inspiration from plants and other biological entities. For instance, some control algorithms are designed to optimize resource allocation and distribution in a manner similar to how plants efficiently allocate nutrients to different parts of their structure. These principles can be applied to manage resources in smart grids, water distribution networks, and other infrastructure systems.

In the field of healthcare, bioinspired controllers have been used to develop wearable devices that monitor physiological signals and provide timely feedback or interventions. These systems can mimic the feedback loops and regulatory mechanisms found in the human body, offering a more natural and effective way to manage health conditions.

Bioinspired innovations in controllers have opened up new possibilities in a wide range of applications, offering solutions that are adaptive, efficient, and robust. By taking inspiration from nature's wealth of solutions to complex problems, these controllers have the potential to revolutionize various industries and make our technology more intelligent and responsive to its environment.

Bioinspired innovations in– Communications

Bioinspired innovations in communications have gained significant attention in recent years, as researchers and engineers look to nature for inspiration to enhance and revolutionize the way we transmit and receive information. By drawing from the remarkable solutions that have evolved in the natural world over billions of years, bioinspired communication technologies offer the potential for more efficient, reliable, and sustainable methods of information exchange.

One of the most intriguing aspects of bioinspired communication is the application of swarm intelligence, which takes inspiration from the collective behaviour of social animals such as bees, ants, and birds. These creatures exhibit remarkable coordination and decision-making abilities as they communicate with each other to achieve common goals, such as finding food sources or defending their colonies. In the world of communications, this concept has been applied to the development of wireless sensor networks, where individual devices work together as a coordinated swarm, adapting and optimizing their communication strategies in response to changing conditions. These networks can self-organize, repair themselves, and efficiently transmit data, making them highly robust and adaptable.

Biological organisms have also inspired advances in the design of network topologies. For instance, the structure of neural networks in the human brain has led to the development of artificial neural networks in the field of deep learning, which have proven to be highly effective in tasks like image and speech recognition. The brain's interconnected neurons and their ability to transmit information efficiently have inspired researchers to design artificial systems that mimic these natural structures, enabling more sophisticated and versatile communication capabilities.

Furthermore, the study of animal sensory systems has provided insights into developing communication technologies that are more resilient and adaptable. For example, the echolocation systems of bats and dolphins have inspired the creation of radar and sonar systems used in various applications, from military and navigation to medical imaging. These systems emit signals and interpret the returning echoes to gather information about the surrounding environment. By mimicking these biological systems, engineers have developed advanced communication tools that operate effectively even in challenging environments, such as in underwater or remote areas.

Bioinspired innovations have also made an impact in the field of optical communication. The iridescent properties of certain butterfly wings have inspired the development of new materials that can manipulate and control light for more efficient optical data transmission. Researchers have created photonic crystals and met materials that can manipulate the properties of light, allowing for the design of smaller and faster optical communication devices.

Moreover, the quest for energy-efficient communication technologies has led to the study of energy-efficient systems in nature. Birds, for instance, optimize their flight paths to conserve energy during migration. This concept has been applied to routing algorithms in wireless communication networks, where data is transmitted along paths that minimize energy consumption. By emulating nature's energy-efficient strategies, we can reduce the carbon footprint of communication networks and make them more environmentally friendly.

bioinspired innovations in communications offer a wealth of opportunities to improve the efficiency, adaptability, and sustainability of our information exchange systems. By drawing from nature's solutions, we can create technologies that are more robust, energy-efficient, and versatile, ultimately leading to advancements that benefit various sectors, from healthcare and transportation to environmental monitoring and beyond.

Bioinspired innovations in– Healthcare

Bioinspired innovations in healthcare have emerged as a dynamic field that draws inspiration from nature to develop novel solutions to complex medical challenges. By studying biological systems, organisms, and their intricate mechanisms, scientists and engineers have been able to create innovative medical technologies, treatments, and diagnostics. These bioinspired approaches not only improve patient care but also contribute to sustainable, efficient, and minimally invasive healthcare solutions. Here, we explore several key areas where bio inspiration has made significant contributions to the healthcare industry.

Biomimetic Materials: Nature has provided a wealth of inspiration for developing advanced materials used in healthcare. For example, the structure of seashells has inspired the creation of strong and lightweight materials for bone implants, while the properties of spider silk have been leveraged to design biocompatible wound dressings. These biomimetic materials mimic nature's characteristics, such as strength, flexibility, and biodegradability, to enhance the durability and compatibility of medical devices.

Drug Delivery Systems: Many organisms have evolved intricate mechanisms for delivering substances within their bodies. Scientists have drawn inspiration from these systems to design more effective and targeted drug delivery systems. For instance, liposomal drug carriers, modelled after cell membranes, can encapsulate medications and release them in a controlled manner. This approach minimizes side effects and increases the efficiency of drug treatments.

Biomechanics and Prosthetics: The study of animal locomotion and musculoskeletal systems has led to remarkable advances in prosthetic design. Prosthetic limbs now use biomimetic approaches to replicate the natural movement of the human body. This has not only improved mobility and comfort for amputees but has also enhanced their quality of life.

Biologically-Inspired Sensors: Bioinspired sensors mimic the exceptional sensory capabilities found in various species. For instance, technologies that replicate the electroreception abilities of sharks are being developed for early detection of cancer. These sensors can detect minute electrical changes in the body associated with tumour growth, offering a non-invasive diagnostic tool.

Organ Regeneration: Regrowing tissues and organs is a significant challenge in healthcare. Scientists have looked to nature's regenerative abilities for inspiration. Stem cell therapies, which mimic the regenerative potential of certain organisms, show promise in repairing damaged tissues and organs. Furthermore, 3D bio printing technology aims to construct functional tissues by emulating the layer-by-layer building process observed in biological growth.

Antibacterial Strategies: As antibiotic resistance becomes a growing concern, researchers are turning to nature's antimicrobial strategies. The study of compounds produced by marine organisms, such as sponges and corals, has led to the development of new antibiotics. Similarly, the lotus leaf's self-cleaning properties have inspired the creation of antibacterial surfaces, reducing the risk of hospital-acquired infections.

Behavioural and Cognitive Insights: Observing animal behaviour and cognitive processes has provided valuable insights for addressing mental health issues. Bioinspired therapies draw from animal models to develop interventions for conditions like post-traumatic stress disorder (PTSD) and anxiety disorders.

Environmental Monitoring: Nature's precision and adaptability have influenced the development of environmental monitoring technologies. Biomimetic sensors, inspired by the navigation and sensory abilities of birds and insects, aid in tracking air quality, detecting pollutants, and predicting environmental changes that impact public health.

Bioinspired innovations continue to advance healthcare by harnessing the wisdom of nature to address complex medical challenges. These innovations not only enhance the effectiveness of treatments and diagnostics but also contribute to more sustainable and patient-centric healthcare practices. As research in this field progresses, we can anticipate even more breakthroughs that will further revolutionize the healthcare industry.

Bioinspired innovations in– Agriculture

Bioinspired innovations in agriculture have gained considerable attention in recent years as researchers and farmers alike look for sustainable and efficient solutions to address the challenges of modern farming. By drawing inspiration from nature and the intricate mechanisms that have evolved over millions of years, these innovations aim to optimize agricultural practices, reduce environmental impact, and increase crop yields. Here, we explore some key areas where bioinspired approaches are making a significant impact in agriculture.

Precision Farming and Sensing: Many animals, such as bats and dolphins, use echolocation to navigate and locate prey. Similarly, in agriculture, bioinspired technologies have led to the development of sensor systems that mimic natural processes. Drones equipped with advanced sensors and machine learning algorithms can assess crop health and identify areas requiring specific treatments, optimizing resource use and minimizing chemical inputs. These systems, inspired by the precision of nature, enable farmers to make informed decisions and conserve resources.

Biomimetic Crop Protection: Insects have evolved various mechanisms for self-defence, from camouflage to chemical deterrents. By studying these natural strategies, researchers have developed innovative pest control methods. For instance, the use of pheromones to disrupt insect mating patterns, inspired by the communication methods of some insects, can reduce the need for chemical pesticides. Additionally, crops engineered to produce insect-repelling compounds draw inspiration from the protective mechanisms of certain plants.

Soil Health and Mycorrhizal Networks: Mycorrhizal fungi form symbiotic relationships with plants, aiding in nutrient uptake and water absorption. Inspired by these natural partnerships, scientists have developed soil management techniques that encourage the growth of beneficial fungi in agricultural soils. These networks enhance nutrient availability and overall plant health while reducing the need for synthetic fertilizers.

Crop Biomimicry: The design of crop varieties that mimic certain characteristics of wild plants is another bioinspired approach. For instance, some wild grasses can thrive in harsh conditions and low water availability. By studying the genetic traits responsible for their resilience, researchers can develop crop varieties that are more drought-tolerant and better suited to challenging environments.

Pollination and Bee-Inspired Robotics: Declining bee populations have raised concerns about pollination in agriculture. Bioinspired innovations have led to the creation of robotic pollinators, modelled after bees and other pollinators. These autonomous devices can aid in pollination, ensuring the continued productivity of crops.

Vertical Farming and Biomimetic Architecture: Vertical farming takes inspiration from the efficient spatial organization seen in forests and ecosystems. By stacking crops in vertically designed structures, this method maximizes space utilization, conserves resources, and minimizes the need for large areas of farmland. The design of these structures often mimics the natural forms found in ecosystems, optimizing sunlight exposure and airflow for better plant growth.

Aquaponics and Closed-Loop Ecosystems: Aquaponics systems draw inspiration from aquatic ecosystems, where fish waste is used to fertilize plants, and plant roots help purify the water. These closed-loop systems are sustainable, reduce waste, and efficiently produce both fish and crops.

Bioinspired innovations in agriculture are a testament to the remarkable adaptability and resource-efficiency found in nature. By emulating the solutions developed through millions of years of evolution, we can create more sustainable, resilient, and productive agricultural systems that address the challenges of the 21st century while minimizing the environmental impact of farming practices. These innovations not only benefit farmers but also contribute to the global effort to ensure food security and protect our planet's natural resources.

<u>Bioinspired innovations in– food production</u>

Bioinspired innovations in food production have gained increasing attention and significance as the world faces growing challenges related to food security, sustainability, and resource efficiency. Drawing inspiration from nature, researchers and engineers are exploring various ways to enhance and optimize food production systems. These innovations often capitalize on the remarkable adaptability, efficiency, and resilience of biological systems. Here are some notable examples of bioinspired solutions in food production:

Vertical Farming: Taking a cue from the way plants grow in forests, vertical farming systems mimic natural ecosystems by stacking plants in vertical layers. This approach maximizes the use of space and resources while minimizing the environmental impact of traditional horizontal agriculture. Controlled environments with optimized light, humidity, and nutrient delivery systems are designed to simulate ideal growth conditions.

Aquaponics and Closed-Loop Systems: Inspired by the symbiotic relationships in aquatic ecosystems, Aquaponics combines aquaculture (fish farming) and hydroponics (soilless plant cultivation). This approach creates a closed-loop system where fish waste provides nutrients for plants, while the plants help purify the water for the fish. It's a highly efficient method of food production that minimizes waste and resource consumption.

Biomimetic Packaging: Reducing food waste is a crucial aspect of sustainable food production. Biomimetic packaging solutions draw inspiration from nature's ability to protect and preserve biological materials. Examples include coatings that mimic the self-cleaning properties of lotus leaves or the antimicrobial properties of shark skin, which can extend the shelf life of perishable foods.

Insect Farming: Entomophagy, the practice of consuming insects, is an age-old tradition in many cultures. Insects are highly efficient at converting organic matter into protein and other valuable nutrients. Innovators are developing insect farming systems, inspired by the way ants or termites maintain colonies, to produce protein-rich food sources with a minimal environmental footprint.

Bioengineered Crops: Genetic modification of crops has drawn inspiration from the way some plants resist pests or adapt to challenging environmental conditions. By incorporating traits from hardy, pest-resistant, or drought-tolerant plants, scientists are developing bioengineered crops that can thrive in adverse conditions, leading to increased yields and reduced pesticide use.

Ecosystem Modelling for Precision Agriculture: Ecosystems in nature have complex interrelationships between species that promote balance and resilience. In precision agriculture, similar principles are applied by using advanced data analytics and technology to optimize crop management. This helps reduce resource usage, increase crop yield, and minimize environmental impacts.

Algae-Based Food Production: Algae have an impressive growth rate and can be cultivated using minimal resources. Bioinspired solutions in algae farming, like mimicking the way coral reefs efficiently capture sunlight, are being explored for sustainable production of ingredients for various food products, including plant-based alternatives.

Bees and Pollination: Pollinators, such as bees, play a crucial role in agriculture. Innovations inspired by natural pollination processes, like biomimetic drones, are being developed to address pollinator decline and ensure efficient pollination of crops.

Waste Utilization: Nature recycles and repurposes waste efficiently. In the context of food production, this involves finding innovative ways to utilize food waste and by-products to create new products, like converting food scraps into value-added ingredients or animal feed.

Bioinspired innovations in food production are a promising avenue to address the global challenges of feeding a growing population while reducing the environmental impact of agriculture. By drawing inspiration from the resilience and efficiency of natural systems, researchers and engineers are pioneering solutions that can make food production more sustainable and resource-efficient. These innovations hold the potential to transform the way we produce, package, and distribute food, contributing to a more resilient and sustainable future for food systems.

Bioinspired innovations in– Sports

Bioinspired innovations in sports have revolutionized the way athletes train, compete, and even recover from injuries. By drawing inspiration from the natural world, scientists, engineers, and athletes have created cutting-edge technologies and strategies that enhance performance, reduce the risk of injuries, and improve overall sports experiences. These innovations are a testament to the power of biomimicry, where nature serves as a source of inspiration and a blueprint for human ingenuity in the field of sports.

Running like a Cheetah:

One of the most iconic examples of bioinspired innovations in sports is the development of running shoe technology. Shoe designers have drawn inspiration from the cheetah, the fastest land animal, to create highly specialized footwear. Features like lightweight materials, specially designed traction patterns, and cushioning systems inspired by the cheetah's paw pads and leg anatomy have revolutionized the running shoe industry. These advancements enable athletes to achieve better speed, agility, and performance while reducing the risk of injuries.

Swimming Like a Shark:

Swimmers have long been fascinated by the streamlined efficiency of sharks in water. By studying the skin of sharks and their unique dermal dentils, researchers have developed swimsuit materials that mimic the texture and hydrodynamic properties of shark skin. These suits reduce drag and improve buoyancy, helping swimmers glide through the water with minimal resistance. Michael Phelps' famous sharkskin-inspired swimsuit is a prominent example of how bio inspiration has reshaped competitive swimming.

Bionic Limbs:

Amputees and athletes with disabilities have benefited significantly from bioinspired innovations. The development of bionic limbs, inspired by the remarkable adaptability of animal limbs, has enabled athletes to compete at the highest levels. These prosthetics incorporate lightweight materials, advanced sensors, and cutting-edge control systems to provide enhanced mobility and athletic performance. The design of such prosthetics often takes inspiration from the anatomy and mechanics of animals like cheetahs and eagles.

Sportswear Inspired by Beetles:

The Namib Desert beetle's ability to collect water from the air in one of the driest places on Earth has inspired the creation of innovative sportswear fabrics. By mimicking the beetle's bumpy shell structure, scientists have developed materials that can efficiently manage moisture, keeping athletes cool and dry during intense physical activities. These bioinspired fabrics have found applications in sportswear, enhancing comfort and performance for athletes.

Impact-Resistant Helmets:

Concussions and head injuries are a significant concern in many sports. Football, for example, has seen the development of helmets inspired by the woodpecker, a bird known for its ability to withstand high-impact forces when drumming on trees. These helmets incorporate shock-absorbing materials and structural designs inspired by the woodpecker's head to reduce the risk of head injuries in contact sports.

Sports Nutrition Inspired by Ants:

Endurance athletes, such as long-distance runners and cyclists, have benefited from bioinspired innovations in sports nutrition. Ants, known for their ability to carry heavy loads for long distances, have inspired research into how they efficiently convert food into energy. This knowledge has influenced the development of energy gels and drinks that help athletes maintain their stamina during prolonged activities.

Bioinspired innovations in sports continue to evolve, driven by a deep appreciation for the elegance and efficiency of nature's designs. These innovations not only enhance athletic performance but also contribute to the well-being and safety of athletes, ultimately enriching the world of sports and the experiences of both professional and recreational athletes. By learning from the natural world, we can unlock new possibilities and achieve remarkable feats in sports.

Bioinspired innovations in– Environment infrastructure

Bioinspired innovations in environmental infrastructure involve drawing inspiration from nature to design and develop solutions that address various environmental challenges. By emulating the efficiency, resilience, and sustainability found in the natural world, these innovations aim to create infrastructure systems that are not only environmentally friendly but also highly functional. Here are some key examples of bioinspired innovations in environmental infrastructure:

Biomimetic Building Design: Architects and engineers are increasingly looking to nature for inspiration in building design. For instance, biomimetic facades can imitate the self-cleaning abilities of lotus leaves to reduce maintenance and cleaning costs. Biomimicry also offers solutions to improve energy efficiency, such as designing buildings that adapt their ventilation systems based on the principles of termite mound airflow.

Green Infrastructure: Natural ecosystems have been serving as models for green infrastructure projects. Urban planners and engineers mimic the functions of wetlands, forests, and meadows to manage storm water, improve air quality, and reduce the urban heat island effect. Bioinspired storm water management systems, such as bio swales and green roofs, are being increasingly integrated into urban environments.

Biomimetic Materials: The development of materials that mimic natural substances has led to environmentally friendly and sustainable innovations. For instance, bioinspired composites are designed to be lightweight, strong, and durable, drawing inspiration from the structure of materials found in seashells, bones, or plant fibres. These materials can be used in construction and infrastructure projects to reduce environmental impact.

Energy Efficiency: Bioinspired solutions are helping to improve the energy efficiency of environmental infrastructure. Wind turbine designs inspired by humpback whale fins, for example, are more efficient and quieter.

Additionally, studying the flight patterns of birds has informed the development of more aerodynamic and fuel-efficient designs for aircraft and wind turbines.

Wastewater Treatment: Microorganisms in natural ecosystems play a crucial role in breaking down pollutants. Engineers are exploring the use of bioinspired wastewater treatment systems that mimic the purification processes found in wetlands and marshes. These systems can help remove contaminants from water while minimizing the need for chemicals.

Renewable Energy Generation: Solar panels inspired by the structure of leaves and photosynthesis processes are being developed to enhance the efficiency of energy capture. By emulating nature's approach to converting sunlight into energy, these technologies can contribute to a more sustainable energy infrastructure.

Transportation and Mobility: The study of animal locomotion has influenced the design of more efficient and eco-friendly transportation systems. Biomimetic vehicles, such as streamlined trains modelled after the beak of kingfishers, are designed to reduce energy consumption and enhance speed.

Ecosystem Restoration: Restoring damaged ecosystems with bioinspired methods can help improve environmental infrastructure. Projects that mimic natural succession and the interactions of various species can accelerate the recovery of degraded lands and waters, providing benefits for both the environment and local communities.

Bioinspired innovations in environmental infrastructure are not only environmentally responsible but also economically viable. By drawing from the rich resource of nature's design and engineering solutions, we can create infrastructure that is more in harmony with the environment and better equipped to address the challenges of a rapidly changing world. These innovations offer a promising path towards a more sustainable and resilient future for our built environment.

<u>Bioinspired innovations in– Carbon Neutral Solutions (Coral Reefs, Eco-cements)</u>

Bioinspired innovations in the realm of carbon-neutral solutions have garnered significant attention as humanity grapples with the pressing need to mitigate climate change. Two prominent examples of these innovations are inspired by nature's remarkable ecosystems and materials: coral reefs and eco-cements. These innovations offer promising strategies to reduce carbon emissions and enhance sustainability.

Coral Reefs: Nature's Blueprint for Carbon Neutrality

Coral reefs, often referred to as "rainforests of the sea," have provided inspiration for carbon-neutral solutions due to their remarkable ability to sequester carbon and thrive in a balanced ecosystem. Scientists and engineers have been looking to replicate the principles of coral reefs in various ways to combat climate change.

Blue Carbon Sequestration: Coral reefs store vast amounts of carbon through a process known as "blue carbon sequestration." These ecosystems capture and store carbon dioxide in their calcium carbonate structures, effectively removing carbon from the atmosphere. Researchers are exploring the development of carbon capture and utilization (CCU) technologies inspired by coral reefs to sequester carbon on a large scale, potentially aiding in the reduction of atmospheric CO_2 levels.

Eco-friendly Building Materials: The structure and resilience of coral reefs have inspired innovations in eco-friendly building materials. Bio-inspired materials that mimic the properties of coral skeletons, such as their lightweight and strong structure, are being explored for sustainable construction. These materials not only reduce carbon emissions during production but also contribute to energy-efficient and durable buildings.

Eco-Cements: Sustainable Construction through Biomimicry

Eco-cements are another noteworthy bioinspired innovation in the pursuit of carbon-neutral solutions. Traditional cement production is notorious for its high carbon footprint, making it a significant contributor to greenhouse gas emissions. However, eco-cements draw inspiration from nature to create more sustainable alternatives.

Bio mineralization: Nature offers insights into bio mineralization processes where living organisms create mineral structures. Researchers are developing eco-cements that mimic these processes to reduce energy consumption during production. By harnessing the principles of biological mineralization, these materials can be produced with significantly lower carbon emissions.

Self-healing Capabilities: Inspired by the regenerative abilities of certain organisms in nature, eco-cements are designed with self-healing capabilities. This means that cracks and damages in structures made from eco-cement can repair themselves, reducing maintenance and increasing the lifespan of buildings and infrastructure.

Bioinspired innovations in carbon-neutral solutions, such as those drawing inspiration from coral reefs and eco-cements, hold great promise in addressing climate change and promoting sustainability. By emulating the efficiency and resilience of natural ecosystems and materials, these innovations have the potential to reduce carbon emissions, conserve resources, and create a more environmentally friendly future. They represent a harmonious blend of human ingenuity and nature's wisdom, working together to combat one of the greatest challenges of our time.

Bioinspired innovations in– Carbon Free Solutions (Lotus leaf inspired paints)

Bioinspired innovations have increasingly played a pivotal role in the quest for carbon-free solutions, with one intriguing example being the development of lotus leaf-inspired paints. Drawing inspiration from the natural world, particularly the self-cleaning properties of lotus leaves, scientists and engineers have sought to replicate these characteristics in materials and coatings to address various environmental and sustainability challenges.

The lotus leaf, known for its remarkable ability to repel water and stay clean in muddy environments, has a surface covered with microscopic structures that create a unique hydrophobic effect. These structures reduce the contact area between water droplets and the leaf's surface, allowing them to roll off effortlessly, carrying away dirt and contaminants. This "lotus effect" has served as a source of inspiration for the development of super hydrophobic and self-cleaning coatings in the pursuit of carbon-free solutions.

Lotus leaf-inspired paints, also known as super hydrophobic coatings, have found applications in numerous industries and have the potential to contribute to a more sustainable future. Here are some key aspects of their significance:

Water Conservation: The super hydrophobic properties of lotus-inspired paints can be applied to various surfaces, including building materials, to create self-cleaning facades. This reduces the need for frequent washing and maintenance, ultimately conserving water resources.

Energy Efficiency: By reducing the accumulation of dirt and contaminants on surfaces, lotus-inspired paints can help maintain the energy efficiency of solar panels and other energy-harvesting systems. Cleaner surfaces allow for greater light absorption and energy generation, contributing to carbon-free energy production.

Anti-Pollution: In urban environments, air pollution can lead to the accumulation of particulate matter on buildings and infrastructure. Lotus-inspired coatings can resist dirt and pollutants, helping to keep urban areas cleaner and reducing the need for frequent cleaning, which often involves energy-intensive processes.

Marine Applications: The development of lotus leaf-inspired marine paints has the potential to reduce biofouling on ship hulls. By preventing the attachment of marine organisms and barnacles, these coatings can improve the hydrodynamics of ships, reducing fuel consumption and greenhouse gas emissions.

Water Repellency: Beyond self-cleaning properties, these coatings can also offer enhanced water repellency for textiles, preventing moisture from penetrating and thereby enhancing the durability of outdoor clothing and equipment.

However, it is important to note that while lotus-inspired paints offer promising benefits, there are still challenges to overcome. The longevity of these coatings, their environmental impact, and cost-effectiveness are all areas of on-going research and development.

Bioinspired innovations, such as lotus leaf-inspired paints, hold significant potential in the quest for carbon-free solutions. By emulating nature's solutions to water and dirt resistance, these coatings contribute to water conservation, energy efficiency, pollution reduction, and more sustainable practices across various industries. Their evolution continues as researchers work to improve their performance, durability, and eco-friendliness, making them a promising avenue for reducing our environmental footprint and moving towards a more sustainable future.

Bioinspired innovations in– ecorestorations (Eco-friendly pesticide).

Bioinspired innovations in Eco restorations, particularly in the development of eco-friendly pesticides, are revolutionizing the way we approach environmental conservation and sustainable agriculture. Drawing inspiration from nature, these innovations seek to address the critical challenges of restoring ecosystems and protecting crops while minimizing harm to the environment.

One notable example of bioinspired innovation in Eco restorations is the development of bio pesticides. These environmentally friendly pesticides are inspired by natural predators and parasites found in ecosystems. For instance, the use of ladybugs, which are natural predators of aphids, as a bio pesticide, has been highly effective in controlling aphid infestations in agricultural fields. By harnessing the power of nature's own checks and balances, bio pesticides reduce the need for synthetic chemicals that can harm beneficial insects, contaminate soil and water, and pose risks to human health.

Another fascinating bioinspired approach in Eco restorations is the use of pheromones to disrupt the mating behaviours of insect pests. This concept is derived from the way certain insects communicate and reproduce in their natural habitats. By releasing synthetic pheromones, scientists can confuse pests, preventing them from finding mates and reproducing. This approach has proven to be highly specific and effective, reducing the need for broad-spectrum chemical pesticides.

In addition to bio pesticides and pheromones, researchers have looked to nature to develop eco-friendly alternatives to traditional herbicides. One such innovation involves the use of cover crops, which mimic the natural ground cover provided by diverse plant species in healthy ecosystems. These cover crops help suppress weed growth, reduce the need for chemical herbicides, and enhance soil health by adding organic matter.

Furthermore, the concept of "biomimicry" has influenced the development of environmentally friendly coatings and films that can protect crops from pests and diseases. Inspired by the self-defence mechanisms of plants and animals, these coatings are designed to repel or inhibit the attachment of pests and pathogens, reducing the reliance on chemical treatments.

Bioinspired innovations in Eco restorations and eco-friendly pesticides are not only more sustainable but also align with the principles of integrated pest management (IPM). IPM emphasizes a holistic approach to pest control, considering ecological, economic, and social aspects while minimizing the negative impacts of pesticides. By drawing inspiration from the intricate relationships and strategies found in nature, these innovations offer a promising path forward for more sustainable and environmentally responsible pest management practices. As we continue to face the challenges of global food security and environmental conservation, bioinspired solutions in Eco restorations will play an increasingly vital role in addressing these complex issues.

A New Frontier In Design And Innovation

As we reach the end of this journey through the world of bio-inspired design and innovation, it is clear that the possibilities are vast and transformative. The ideas presented in this book are just the beginning of a much larger conversation—one that challenges us to rethink how we create, design, and interact with the world around us. By drawing inspiration from nature's time-tested solutions, we are not only unlocking new ways to solve pressing global challenges, but we are also reconnecting with the deeper intelligence of the natural world that has long been our guide and teacher.

Bio-inspired design is, at its core, an invitation to look at nature with fresh eyes. It encourages us to ask questions that go beyond traditional engineering and design paradigms: How does nature achieve balance. How does it use minimal resources to create maximum impact. What can we learn from the adaptive systems that have allowed life on Earth to thrive for billions of years. These are the questions that drive the innovation we need for a sustainable and harmonious future.

Throughout the chapters of this book, we have explored a diverse range of bio-inspired innovations, from architectural marvels to cutting-edge technologies. These examples serve as a testament to the power of nature's principles when applied thoughtfully to human problems. Yet, as we've seen, bio-inspired design is still in its early stages. There is so much more to discover—new materials, new designs, and new ways of thinking that will continue to shape the future.

It is my hope that this book has sparked your curiosity and inspired you to explore further the many ways in which we can apply the wisdom of nature to our modern challenges. Whether you are a designer, engineer, researcher, or simply someone passionate about sustainability, there are countless opportunities for collaboration and innovation at the intersection of biology and design. The journey ahead will require creativity, bold thinking, and a commitment to learning from the natural world in ways that are both respectful and innovative.

As you move forward, I encourage you to ask yourself: How can we design in harmony with nature. What new possibilities can we discover by observing the world around us with a sense of wonder and curiosity. The answers are waiting, just beyond the horizon.

Bio-inspired design is not just a trend—it is a movement, a new way of thinking that holds the potential to redefine how we build, create, and live. It is a way forward that can help us reconnect with the Earth, address the challenges of sustainability, and build systems that are both innovative and resilient.

The future of design is bio-inspired, and it is ours to shape.

Shiva Prakash .S
Senior Assistant professor
New Horizon College of engineering
Bangalore